the spare-time gardener

the spare-time gardener

Tips and Tricks for Those on the Go

Barbara Hill Freeman

Illustrations by
Abigail Brooke Allison and
Barbara Hill Freeman

taylor trade publishing

Lanham • New York • Boulder • Toronto • Oxford

Published by Taylor Trade Publishing
An imprint of The Rowman & Littlefield Publishing Group, Inc.
4501 Forbes Boulevard, Suite 200, Lanham, Maryland 20706

Distributed by NATIONAL BOOK NETWORK

Library of Congress Cataloging-in-Publication Data

Freeman, Barbara Hill, 1947–
    The spare-time gardener : tips and tricks for those on the go / Barbara Hill Freeman.—
1st Taylor Trade Pub. ed.
        p. cm.
    Includes index.
    ISBN-10: 1-58979-188-6 (pbk. : alk. paper)
    ISBN-13: 978-1-58979-188-6
    1. Gardening. I. Title.
SB453.F74 2006
635—dc22
                                                                            2005024581

contents

Part Three

time to get growing

Part Four

keep growing in your spare time

Part Five

garden odds and ends

acknowledgments

Plants give us so much. They provide beauty, of course; but they also clean our air and cool our environment. They offer shade and shelter. They appeal to all our senses. People who garden have an uncanny connection to the green world. They know and understand plants. They speak Plant.

My plant-obsessed family, friends, and colleagues have been a source of inspiration, as well as information.

Thanks to botanist and friend Lauren Stockwell, who asked if I knew anyone who'd like to write a gardening book. "Yes, I would," was my immediate reply. She put me in touch with the Allen O'Shea Literary Agency, which led to my association with Marilyn Allen, who possesses just the right combination of enthusiasm, skill, good humor, and patience. The horticulturists, botanists, and just plain enthusiasts associated with Coastal Maine Botanical Gardens offer an endless stream of gardening wisdom born of years of study and experience. Most gardeners are like that; they want to share what they know. Pat Jeremiah is generous in communicating her tremendous store of practical and often arcane gardening knowledge; and she and Janice Serencko help keep me relatively sane. Dick Zieg and Bruce McElroy know all about practical gardening techniques and like to help the rest of us get it right. John Manion revels in his knowledge of the world of plants and loves to share it. Maureen Heffernan—the boss—knows all about gardens and gardening. Thanks also to Ginger Carr, Dr. Elsie Freeman, and Marjorie Van Voorhis, whose home landscapes express perfectly their dedication to the art of gardening. They readily shared their favorite tips, plant names, and tools.

Mark Hutchinson and Liz Stanley with the University of Maine Cooperative Extension quite obviously believe that the world revolves around growing and gardening. That kind of fervor is catching, and I've succumbed. Bob Boyd and his employees at Boothbay Region Greenhouses are a model for what the people who run a nursery should be: they're helpful and knowledgeable, and they're good listeners, too.

There's been encouragement on the home front, too. One snowy March day as I was typing merrily away, thinking green thoughts, our building contractor, Eric Marden, and a carpenter were tearing into the kitchen walls with crowbars. Another couple of guys were hammering away at the roof, having just removed the latest foot of snow in what was a very nasty winter; and two men I'd never seen before donned "space suits" and set about dislodging a square of asbestos left over when the antiquated oil burner was removed.

The renovation work on our old Maine cottage went on for several months. In the makeshift office, surrounded by boxes holding the contents of the old kitchen, I wrote as the dog and cats napped—all of us seeking refuge from the commotion and destruction. Whenever I'd cautiously venture out to see how the project was progressing, the builders would ask in their genial Downeast way, "How's the book coming, dee-ah?" These pages will forever be associated in my mind with my new, long-awaited kitchen.

Any husband who can put up with that kind of chaos and still encourage his wife to let the wallboard dust collect and let him cook the frozen meals while she writes about the fluffy subject of gardening is a gem indeed. Ned, "The Mad Pruner," is just such a husband, and I'm immensely grateful for his support and ideas. He approaches garden chores with gusto, and it was he who suggested a chapter called "Plant Me Now!"

My son and daughter, Zack Shenkle and Abbey Allison, both think working on a gardening book is a good antidote for writing press releases and newsletters. As usual, they're right. And thinking of gardens and gardening certainly kept me from becoming totally mired in the details of planning Abbey and Shawn's wedding. Watching Shawn Allison's concentration as he composes music is an inspiration to me as I compose in words. May Shawn and Abbey long make beautiful music together—literally.

Thanks, finally, to the good people at the Rowman & Littlefield Publishing Group. They recognized that spare-time gardeners deserve a book that can encourage them to get great results by doing as much as they can . . . and no more than they want to.

And thank you for reading this book. I hope you like it and even learn something new.

introduction

What is spare time anyway? Sure, it's time that's left over after everything that *needs* to be done is done. But spare also means meager, less than plentiful. Is your leftover time, your "spare" time, always way too meager? Of course it is!

That said, let's get on with it. This book is about gardening in whatever time we can eke out, what we laughingly call our spare time. You'll be amazed, though, how tweaking your approach and streamlining your efforts can yield great results in less time.

Gardening is often overcomplicated by experts, almost to the point of mumbo-jumbo. Granted, a lot of talented botanists, horticulturists, and other "ists" have come up with ideas and methods that really stand the test of time; and these practices should be observed and even cherished. Nonetheless, some gardeners seem to have *too much*

time on their hands. They make work for themselves and then find a reason to justify it.

We're not going to do that. The be-all and end-all is to achieve garden nirvana—a place where you're happy with your garden but not too exhausted to enjoy it. To get there, you have to get to know yourself a little better; and you should learn, or review, some gardening basics. You have to dig in the dirt, handle plants with abandon, keep track, and do some watchful waiting.

To glean as much as possible from gardening—a beautiful and enjoyable outdoor space of your own, physical and mental health benefits, newfound knowledge and confidence, the pleasure of planning and planting, and the absolute joy of watching plants flourish—you should start small and watch yourself grow right along with your garden. Although gardening can be hard work, it's better not to approach it as a chore, but rather as an opportunity. It's work with the potential to be immensely satisfying, not to mention lots of fun.

Start small; and when you gain confidence, go a little further and then a little further still until you feel thoroughly at home in your own garden. The spare-time gardener's journey can be as delightful and as rewarding as the results. So, let's get started.

part one

Getting to Know You

I

expectations vs. reality
in the garden

I know you; in fact, we have a lot in common. Each spring, surrounded by glossy plant catalogues and armed with a mental list of all the nurseries within reach, we contemplate our gardens to be. We buy a few plants (okay, a *lot* of plants), some completely new to us, but the pictures and descriptions are so appealing we can't resist them. Sound familiar?

We say to ourselves, "This year I'm going to spend *X* amount of time in the garden each day [you fill in the blank]. I'm going to hit the ground running and keep pace with planting, fertilizing, mowing, and weeding so they don't get ahead of me as they somehow do each year. My yard and garden will be neat and colorful—a welcome refuge and a setting for elegant entertaining and fun-filled days throughout the growing season and beyond, no matter what."

THE SLOUGH OF DESPAIR—GARDEN STYLE

It's a pretty picture. Unfortunately, for all but the most efficient gardeners (or those with full-time help), these goals work in theory, but not in practice. Once reality steps in, the stunning garden in our mind's eye is but a dream for the next year—and the next. The dead foliage of spent spring bulbs lies moldering on top of equally spent soil. Annuals fail to thrive, especially if we never get around to taking them out of their six-packs. Instead of flourishing and increasing in size and vigor, perennials continue a steady decline. Garden furnishings are unsightly and, worse still, unused. And weeds? Well, the weeds simply win the war.

So between the delightful expectation and the bleak reality, what happens? Time happens, or more accurately, the lack of time. We're holding down a job or two and raising a family; or we're retired and traveling, volunteering, etc. There are cooking, cleaning, and maintenance chores to do. The kids or grandchildren are home, but gardening isn't their thing. We take a vacation and return to find a jungle where our yard had been. It's an extra-dry (or extra-wet) season, and nothing wants to grow. Pests or diseases decimate our plants. By the time we get home from work we have neither the time nor energy to get out in the garden, even for that elusive *X* number of minutes or hours. When we do find the time to dig in the dirt, everything takes longer than we expect. With each passing day, we get more and more behind and further and further from our ideal.

I know all these excuses; I've *used* them. To imperfect perfectionists like us, this gulf between expectation and reality is utterly frustrating. By the end of the season, we feel like failures. We're just about ready to give up gar-

dening for good. We find ourselves wondering how the yard would look paved in concrete or covered in green plastic turf.

HERE'S THE GOOD NEWS

The gulf between our gardening dreams and what we achieve can be bridged. First, we need a reality check—a shift in perception. Then we need to learn ways to make gardening easier, faster, more productive, and fun; and there definitely *are* ways! I've discovered them through trial and error, by poring over the 2,000-volume library at the botanical garden where I work, and by talking to experts willing to share their secrets. While I'll provide time-savers and indulge in a bit of philosophizing to make the job less onerous, be forewarned: There's no magic way to a totally labor-free garden—except by hiring the aforementioned full-time help; and how many of us can, or want to, do that?

Then why bother? Because even if the garden gets the better of us time after time, we begin each growing season with renewed enthusiasm and hope. This is a book for optimists. It's more than a how-to; it's about a philosophy of gardening and the enduring pleasure and tangible benefits that come from creating a satisfying personal landscape—in this case, one that takes only the time we have to give it, and is worth every minute.

the spare-time gardener

2

"plant me now!"

At this very moment there are plants and flowers out there simply shouting, "Plant me now!" Just this once, don't think twice. Instead of planning before you plant, start out with a project that appeals to your need for instant gratification. After all, you have a bit of work, both mental and physical, ahead of you; and this is good practice. By rewarding yourself first—before you ever pick up your pencil or spade—you'll be encouraged to go on.

In Psych 101 they call it positive reinforcement. I call it a gift to yourself. It won't take long. It will be easy, fun, and satisfying; and the results will make you want to continue towards the greater and even more satisfying rewards ahead.

Of course, easier still would be to purchase a preplanted container. Go ahead if you must. Buying a ready-made garden in a pot certainly saves time, but it usually costs more than the component parts. More importantly, it deprives you of the fun and pride you'll experience by planting the container yourself and admiring the display for months to come. Instead, why not use the planted containers you see at the nursery as teaching tools and clues to what you can grow?

But how can you inspire yourself to begin gardening, and do it quickly and easily? My husband, Ned, heretofore unrecognized as a major poet, suggests the following: "Get off your duff and plant some stuff."

Here's how.

FIRST: GO SHOPPING

Shopping is always a viable alternative to work—even in the garden. Next time you know you'll be driving by your local garden center or megastore, allow yourself an extra half hour or so to stop by and begin the gift to yourself.

First, look for a sizeable pot that really appeals to you. A top diameter of anywhere from 16 to 20 inches will do nicely. It can be pottery or plastic, terra-cotta or faux, painted or natural. It should have a hole in the bottom for drainage, and it can have features such as an attached saucer, or even a water reservoir to cut down on watering chores. No matter what you buy, it doesn't have to cost a fortune, but you *do* have to like the way it looks.

While you're there, purchase between 9 and 20 plants, depending on their size and the size of your container. Choose more than you think you'll need. Select annuals rather than perennials; we're not going for perpetuity here.

The plants don't have to be huge, but they do have to be different shapes: one to three that are tall and spiky, five to ten medium sized and bushy, and three to seven cascading or vinelike. They also have to be colorful of foliage or flower—or both; and they have to appeal to you since, if you heed my advice, it'll be a little while before you plant much else.

If you're attracted to a pot that's at the upper end of the size range, or even a huge pot, you'll have to bring home either more or bigger plants proportional to the container, as well as more soil.

An aside: If you happen to see, or already have, a small trellis or framework you like, you can substitute climbing vines for the tall plants. Morning glories work nicely, especially the ones that belie their name and bloom throughout the day. Purchase one for each leg of the support and put the plant right by it. Wind the branches around the leg, leaving room for growth.

If possible, once you've selected some plants you like, set their individual pots or packages on the ground or a table all snugged in together to see how they'll look together and approximately how much space they'll take. If that isn't an option, you'll need to use your imagination instead. If you don't like your choices or don't think you have enough plants for the size of the container, now's the time to make changes.

No matter what the container, the object is to fill it liberally and lushly with greenery and blooms. Remember, we're looking for instant gratification— no miserly little displays for us!

While you're at this same store, buy a bag of potting soil—nothing elaborate, but make sure it's marked "sterile," "artificial," or "soilless" and that there's enough of it to fill the pot you've chosen. If you want to cut down on watering, you can try the type that contains bits of polymer that soak up water and then provide it as the soil becomes dry.

Add to your shopping cart a small container of time-release plant food (fertilizer), too. Again, nothing fancy. A little goes a long way towards creating a good and lasting display. Just read the labels and purchase one that promises to promote bloom without the need for frequent application. If you buy a soil that contains fertilizer, you can skip this step.

If your container will be on an outdoor surface that's impervious to water, don't worry about putting a saucer under it. You might want to prop it up a bit, though, to allow the water to drain. Garden centers sell "feet" for just this purpose, or you can improvise.

If, on the other hand, the pot will be on a surface that can't take too much moisture, buy or find a plant saucer that's a couple of inches larger than the plant's bottom diameter. Plastic is probably best because water won't leach through it. Big, round trays or large, flat deli containers from the supermarket work great for larger containers.

Rummaging through your garage may net some of the above supplies. If so, fine. Just don't make it hard on yourself. That defeats the purpose of this exercise.

SIZE UP THE SPACE

When you get your container home, look around for a spot that's sunny most of the day, and where you'll often be able to see and admire your accomplishment. If it's winter and you're in the northern half of the U.S., that spot will probably be inside. Come late spring, you can move the whole show outdoors. I've been growing geraniums (*Pelargonium*), ivies, and herbs that way for years.

Because it's easier to carry an empty container than to lug a full one, jostling plants and spilling soil as you go, it's a good idea to take everything to the area where you want the pot to sit and work on your container garden there. If you're worried about the carpet or the decking, cover the area where you're planting with a large piece of plastic.

Okay, now we're ready to plant.

FILL 'ER UP

To keep soil from leaking out through the drainage hole, take a coffee filter, a piece of newspaper, or some loose stones or shards (pieces of broken pots) and place them in the bottom of the container to cover the hole. If you use shards, position them so water can get under them and out the bottom of the pot. If there's no hole in the container you choose, you can either drill one or several half-inch holes, or you can fill the container a quarter of the way up with small stones or gravel to provide some interior drainage. The latter might be the only option if the pot is

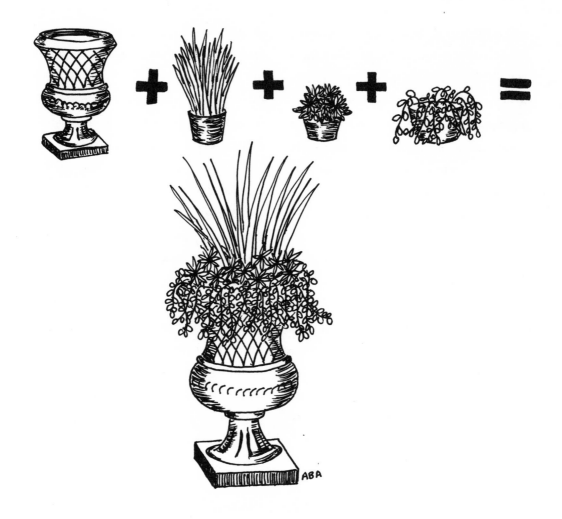

delicate and might split if you try to drill into it.

If the container's big enough or made of a material that makes it likely to be really heavy once it's filled with soil, fill it to about halfway up with something like foam peanuts (loosely encased in a plastic bag to prevent a mess later on!) or rumpled-up bubble wrap.

Then come the soil and fertilizer. Fill the container to within three inches of the top rim, and add a scoop or two of fertilizer (again, read the label), thoroughly mixing it into the soil.

Shake it so the soil filters down around the shards or other filler and then tamp down the surface a little, but don't get carried away. For this kind of work, I seldom wear garden gloves, preferring the feel of the soil and plants; but you might be of a different opinion. If so, just make sure your gloves allow you the dexterity you need.

Now for the plants. Tap each one out of its pot or six-pack as you're ready to use it. Begin by centering the tall one in the pot. Work it in so about an inch of the soil that came with it is still exposed. Then, add the medium-height, bushy plants at equal intervals about halfway between the tall plant and the pot's rim. Finally, closer to the rim, evenly space the vines, positioning them so they drape artfully over the side of the container.

Since the plants themselves all begin about an inch above the soil, we have to fill in around them to bring the soil height up to between one and two inches from the rim. So, take a little more potting soil and, with a trowel or your hands, spread it between the plants so that the surface is even and no roots are exposed.

WATER AND WATCH IT GROW

Water liberally, so the soil is soaked, at least to several inches below the top. With some soil or soilless mixes, this may take several light waterings to accomplish.

Every day or so as the surface begins to dry out, water your container again. Factors that affect how often you'll need to add water include the type and amount of soil mix you're using, the weather, and the size of the pot. This shouldn't be a hardship; just grab a watering can as you're headed towards this convenient and visible spot you've chosen. Since this is also a good project for children, if you have any at home, why not enlist their help in maintaining your container garden?

Although the point of packing plants into the container is to make it look great from day one, your plants will grow and prosper and look even fuller as the season progresses. And you'll be inspired.

You've just given yourself a wonderful present. You've allowed yourself to plant a small but beautiful garden using only what appeals to you and, most importantly, without stress and strain. Because of the way you went about this project, you'll appreciate the results all the more. Pull up a chair and enjoy the show.

Now, just imagine what you can accomplish with a little more effort. Read on.

3

"plant me next!"

Now that you have a container garden under your belt, you're ready for something bigger—a flower bed. The following chapters will give you information you need to get started on a landscape plan. Then you'll proceed to a planting plan and purchasing, planting, and growing your plants. The container was great practice, but now you're facing the prospect of planting and maintaining your entire property.

If you want to avoid feeling overwhelmed at this gardening game, don't try to finish or even begin your whole project at once. Start with one small garden you can build in a weekend's worth of spare time, and then progress to the next and the next as you have time and resources.

If it begins to get out of hand and you run out of time, sit back and reexamine your ideas and actions. You might be overcomplicating your gar-

dening chores, or the landscape plan you've created might be too elaborate— or you might just need more time to get it all done.

To get started on your one, small garden, we'll put aside the finer points for now and just dig and plant and see what happens. We'll assume you already have a few tools. Think of this as an experiment to gauge your time outlay, interest, physical stamina, and other elements and attributes you'll need for more extensive gardening.

BUT WHERE? HOW?

Pick out a sunny spot close to your entry or kitchen door. For our purposes, sunny means six to eight hours a day of sun. Mark off a section no larger than four by eight feet. It can have a gentle curve to it or an oval shape. If it's against a wall or a building, the outer edge can curve away from the structure. Since we're starting from scratch in this one area, ideally it shouldn't contain any plants you want to keep, or at least can't easily move.

If your property has a lot more shade than sun, you can select a partly shady spot and choose plants accordingly. If the only place you want a garden contains a tree or other plants you can't or don't want to move, again, just plan accordingly. Be as flexible as you need to be. Of course it's important to put this little flower and/or herb-vegetable bed where you'll want some garden, any garden—even a bigger one—in the future.

Let's say this new garden backs up to your house. Begin the four-foot measurement just beyond the drip line of the roof. If you're curving the edges, you may go out a little more than four feet from there. Use your artistic sensibilities (you have them, or you wouldn't care about gardening).

Now, you want to clear your artist's canvas. Dig out any grass within this new garden area. If it's next to the house, clear the entire area from the house out to the far edge of the plot. If there are relatively small plants there you want to keep, either work around them or, easier by far, dig them up and put them aside temporarily—even a cardboard box will work for this. Just make sure you include some of the soil around them and keep them moist until you can replant them.

If you want to make the process of removing grass easier but slower, spread plastic over the ground and let the sun beat down on it for a week or so. Everything under the plastic will turn brown and will be a bit easier to dig out. If you want to save any grass and transplant it, more power to you. Dig up your grass in strips or squares. Just remember to create a depression the depth of the sod in the area where you want to put it; that way it will match the area around it.

Now that your garden is empty of plants, use a flat spade or other tool to make a nice, neat edge—a frame for your garden. Dig out any small stones you find and put them in a bucket or box, and rake the soil until it's fairly smooth. Rock makes a great accent in the garden. If there are large stones, you can move them aside temporarily (if they aren't too heavy) and then incorporate them into your garden before you plant. If they're *big*, let them be and work around them.

It's time to take another trip to your local garden center. Using your favorite color as a guide, purchase plants whose flowers are in that color family, are near neighbors, or complement it (blue and white go with everything in the garden, for example). For now, stick with a range of several colors rather than a whole bunch, so the effect will be homogenous.

When making your selections, go with tried-and-true favorites that grow well in your area. You can find out which ones they are by asking the nursery staff. If your new garden is in the shade, then make sure you purchase shade-loving plants. If you'd rather grow vegetables and herbs, follow the same guidelines using different plants and keeping in mind that you'll need to select an area with lots of sun. Combining herbs and vegetables with flowers is a great way to have the best of both worlds.

Your suggested shopping list is as follows:

- Seven tall flowering perennials (height at maturity around three feet). These will become your background planting. Purchase only five if they are, or will grow to be, broad as well as tall (e.g., hydrangea, spirea), nine if they're skinny (e.g., phlox or delphinium). If you want to plant vines (clematis or morning glory), purchase simple stakes or trellises on which they can grow.
- Nine to fifteen medium-height perennials (one to two feet at maturity). These will make up the middle ground in your garden. Again, if they're relatively small or thin species, go with the larger number. If your garden is in the sun, you can include a couple of eggplant or tomato plants in cages to approximate a true kitchen garden.

- Two dozen assorted low annuals in colors that will complement the other plants in the garden. You can add herbs into this mix; they'll add greenery and texture rather than color—and that's just fine. These will become the foreground of your garden, and their colors will add an exclamation point to the display.
- Two large bags of compost
- Two bags of fine or medium bark mulch (the really coarse stuff is hard to handle)
- A container of all-purpose fertilizer as recommended by the garden center (the staff will know the general soil conditions you might have)

PLANT YOUR NEW GARDEN

Now that you're home with your new garden in the trunk of your car (this may take more than one trip!), open the bags of compost and spread this magical material on the area you've dug. Sprinkle on a layer of fertilizer using the amount per square foot as recommended on the container for your 32-square-foot garden bed.

Then, with a spade, mix the compost and fertilizer into the first few inches of soil. Again, rake the surface. Because you've plumped up the soil both by adding the compost to it and digging in it, you'll have a mounded garden with fluffy soil. Try not to walk on it from now on. You won't have to, since if you kneel or stand at the back and front edges of the garden to work on it you'll never have to reach much more than a couple of feet to get to the farthest plants. Do you have a kneeling pad or kneepads? If not, you'll need them soon. For now, though, you can use an old pillow or folded towel you were ready to toss out anyway.

Lay out the pots on your newly dug ground, arranging the tallest plants in back, the medium-height plants in the middle, and the short annuals in front; or, if your garden's an island, taller plants in the middle and the midsized and smaller plants spreading out around them. Stagger the arrangement so it doesn't look regimented, and allow more room around the plants that will grow biggest. Starting with the midsized plants in the middle of the garden (or the tall plants if it's an island), dig holes and plant them so the soil in the pot is even with the soil in which you're planting them. Press gently around each plant, and you'll make a small depression in the soil to hold water.

Proceed to the other plants, packing the annuals as tightly as the number you've purchased will allow. Spread out the tall perennials, while zigzagging them a little, to fit the eight-foot width of the garden.

Next, water your garden thoroughly, which means longer than you'd expect. Once you're quite sure the top several inches of soil are moist (dig a little hole and check), open the bags of mulch and spread the pieces of pine bark or whatever you've selected around the plants, again starting in the middle. Depending on the coarseness of the mulch, two large bags should be enough to cover your garden to a depth of an inch or two. If you have too much, spread it elsewhere in your garden; too little, buy another bag next time you're out running errands.

Now, wipe your brow, have a seat, and admire your work.

This is a good time to take stock, too, which will be helpful as you plan the rest of your garden. How did it feel? Was the work easy or hard? Were you on familiar territory or breaking new ground—so to speak?

4

the space-time continuum, garden style

The more space we have in our garden, the more time it takes to fill it with plants, and then to tend those plants. I'm not suggesting you move to a smaller property, although downsizing has a lot to recommend it. I am suggesting that wherever possible you simplify your gardening efforts. Less truly can be more—more time, more freedom, more savings, and even more pleasure and beauty.

Simplifying isn't always so simple, though. You'll find contradictions and challenges. What can you do to make gardening easier and faster without taking two steps backwards for every step forward? Here are a few basic "rules" to follow and some "buts" to consider:

- Take shortcuts wherever you can, but only if those shortcuts won't make more work later on.

- Get out in the garden as soon as possible when conditions are right, but don't try to do too much the first day—or even the first week. Ease into garden work or the muscles you haven't used for a while will complain mightily, and that will set you back a few days while you wait till you can kneel down and bend again. I always spend hours at gardening the first chance I get and then pay the price; so please do as I say, not as I do.

- Pay attention to what you and your family want from your yard, not what your neighbors, or even your friends, think you should have.

- Use time-saving devices, as long as they don't cost the world, but only if they do indeed save time.

- If you get ideas from glossy magazines and trips to fantastic gardens, great; but don't feel you have to reproduce these picture-book plantings in your own yard. Pick and choose what you like, and try it on a smaller or simpler scale.
- Maintenance is important, but try not to become discouraged if the weeds get the upper hand once in a while. You can take them on when you get the time. After all, you're bigger than they are—*aren't* you?
- Listen to experts' advice, but make up your own mind. It's *your* garden—and your time and money.
- Choose only plants and designs you like. Go with your gut instincts, and your garden is more likely to please you and have staying power.
- Be a selective shopper. Sometimes it's fun and easy to buy plants, tools, and garden accessories by phone or online. When you receive catalogues, whether by post or e-mail, they're full of promise and promises; and there are some things you can only get by ordering them through a catalogue. Learn from them and make selections; but before you send off your hard-earned cash, be sure that what they're offering is right for you and fits into your overall plan. You might even find what you're looking for faster, cheaper, and fresher at the garden center around the corner; but you'll never know till you do a little homework. Comparing your options will pay dividends in time and cash and, in the end, will help you simplify the process.

HOW MUCH TIME, ANYWAY?

Speaking of time, how much of it does any given garden task take? The answer is indubitably and irrevocably "more than you'd think." It's also different for every single individual. When planning time to work in your garden, factor in the following:

- Time to change into your grubbies. Don't forget sturdy, comfortable shoes and socks, as well as a wide-brimmed hat.
- Time to slather on sunscreen (another reason to garden on rainy days) and bug repellent, if it's the season for your least favorite insects
- Time to round up all your tools and supplies (organization helps here)
- Time to drag into the garden the tools, soil, mulch, drinking water,

compost, hose, plants, kneeling pad, *your garden journal,* and anything else you'll need. This is an argument for keeping what you'll use in one place. Searching over, under, and around everything in your garage to find your favorite hand pruner is a frustrating waste of time.

- Time to cultivate the garden and improve the soil
- Time to dig holes and plant the plants
- Time to water, fertilize, and mulch the plants
- Time to pull out any weeds determined enough to break their way through the mulch

- Time to admire and contemplate your colorful, beautiful garden and nature all by yourself
- Time to entertain and share your (and nature's) creation with your family, friends, and neighbors. Don't be afraid to let your pride show. You've earned their accolades. Every occasion to spend time in your garden is a special occasion.

Of course, by no means does every one of the above tasks need to be done every day—or even every week. And you needn't stretch out all these chores, except maybe the most enjoyable, to fill up all the time you can give your garden.

5

evolution of a gardener

In hopes that it will be helpful, I'd like to tell you the story of how I've grown, and continue to grow, into an enthusiastic spare-time gardener. You should know right off, though, that I've been looking for ways to streamline gardening chores ever since I first put trowel to soil. For me, that's part of the challenge, and the fun, of having a garden that looks great without taking all your time, and without breaking your bank or your back.

I was born in Philadelphia, home of one of the finest of those annual garden extravaganzas that keep gardeners sane until spring arrives. My earliest memories of the Philadelphia Flower Show are of looking *up* at the display tables; I was that young. But I didn't give a hoot about plants then. My father, who was from England, was the gardener in our household. My mother joked that when he called from

the road (he was a salesman), he asked how the plants were doing before he asked about us. She was exaggerating only slightly.

Dad was living proof that the British have a flair for gardening. I'm told that, before I was born, he would spend the equivalent of a week's grocery money on what looked like old, dried-up potatoes. They were dahlia bulbs, and he went to great lengths to cultivate them. That's how we came to be at the Philadelphia Flower Show when I was a little tyke, but I'm afraid all that plant pulchritude didn't do much for me.

LABORS OF LOVE

Wherever we lived, on Long Island's Little Neck Bay, in the Philadelphia suburbs, or on a sandy-soiled barrier island in South Jersey, Dad's lush plantings and landscapes were so beautiful that passersby would stop to admire them and sometimes take pictures and even ask for cuttings. Now it can be told: His expansive and much-admired rock garden in Wyncote, Pennsylvania, was built with mica-studded stones "left over" from the construction of the Gimbel's department store just down the road, and lugged home by my father in the trunk of our 1956 Chevy during weekend visits to the site.

Even when I was knee-high to a watering can, and forever after, I was included in the garden workforce. I watered (and was taught that I had to stand in one place endlessly to get enough water on each plant); learned the hard way that garter snakes are harmless; deadheaded and weeded (and could eventually tell "weedlings" from seedlings), dragged around huge bags of the peat moss my father used as mulch (I loved the rich color and smell, but hated the way it floated away before it soaked up enough water to become a sodden mass).

After all that "fun," unbelievable as it may seem, I still wasn't really interested. In spite of myself, though, I had learned a thing or two about gardens and gardening.

FIRST STEPS

Only as I was nearing the end of four years at Boston University did a friend clue me in to the incomparable Thalassa Cruso, a Boston gardening icon who hosted a local TV show with great gusto and wrote wonderful, irreverent books. She's been called the Julia Child of the garden world, and the comparison is apt. I watched for as long as I lived in the area and continued to read her books long afterwards. It began to dawn on me that planting and plants really *could* be fun.

Then, during two years living in a terribly quaint hillside village in southern Germany, I took my first baby step into gardening. Surrounded by verdant mountains and valleys, with a field of potatoes right outside the apartment window and a barn full of cows *under* the house next door, the only way I could join in the rampant ruralness of the place was by planting window boxes. Never mind that our cat, Schneeflocke (snowflake), insisted on sitting amid the portulacas in one pitifully small window box, or that in another the nasturtiums tumbled in every direction but up; it was my first foray into gardening—and it *was* fun.

Back in the States, and back in Philadelphia, I landed a job as administrative assistant to landscape architect Ian McHarg, the "Father of Modern Ecology," and his three partners—not because I knew anything about ecological planning or landscape architecture (or urban planning), but because I was a darned good executive secretary. Lucky for me.

In our Center City office, I was surrounded by professionals who lived and breathed plants. They'd return from trips with bags full of specimens they couldn't wait to show off. On our lunch hours, we'd look at slides of far-off gardens. Any questions I had about my own gardening efforts were answered with assurance and, thankfully, forbearance. Attending the Philadelphia Flower Show's opening was an official duty, with Monday morning quarterbacking afterwards to critique the displays. I had come full circle from those flower shows 20 years before.

At home in a cottage beside the Perkiomen Creek, far from the city, I was within a five-minute walk of one of the East's grandest greenhouses (Ott's) and spent a lot of time there just soaking up the plants' names and learning to recognize them. By then, I'd definitely succumbed, and there was no going back.

On our quarter-acre lot, in soil rich from repeated flooding, I planted a big (*too* big) raised vegetable garden, built a too-ambitious double-bin compost heap, designed special stone planters for the side of the house, planted bulb collections we'd received as gifts, transplanted succulents from my father's garden, and nurtured the hundreds of wildflowers that burst into bloom each spring in our very own alluvial floodplain of a yard—all the time continuing to work in far-off Philly.

Now, it was my garden people were stopping to admire and ask for cuttings from; and, as we say in Maine, I was some proud.

Around that same time, I began visiting botanical gardens. Over the years, I've spent time in dozens of gardens from Europe to New Zealand. In addition to being dazzled by the flowers, displays, and landscaping, I've learned something from each and every one. If you haven't already added botanical gardens to your "must visit" list, now's the time to start. They're among the most beautiful and fascinating attractions you'll find, and they reflect the culture and growing practices of the country and region in which they're located. Besides, the gift shops are almost always outstanding.

After moving from the creek house, I continued to plant and grow gardens at four subsequent houses in Bucks County, Pennsylvania, learning about these properties as I went along—by trial and error and lots of visits to garden centers. Fortunately, previous owners had all been—or hired—crackerjack gardeners, so I inherited great plants and good landscape designs. I was able to learn from their successes.

I helped my children dig endless pumpkin patches and flower beds in these previously perfect yards in a bid to interest them in gardening. Now, finally, in their 20s, they're beginning to awaken to the prospect of greenery in their lives. History does repeat itself.

As a boy, my husband lived in Riverdale, New York, on the estate now known as Wave Hill, which later became a public garden. The magnificent plantings at this property overlooking the Hudson River, with a fine view of the Palisades on the opposite shore, are an inspiration to all who visit—and they certainly have been to me. Walking the grounds and visiting the greenhouse with family or with longtime head gardener Marco Polo Stufano, now retired and still revered, made me want to try new plants and even provided ideas for our own garden design and practices—on a much, much smaller scale.

BREAKING NEW GROUND

Fifteen years ago, we moved from Pennsylvania to the coast of Maine (what *were* we thinking!). It may be just one hardiness zone further north, but what a zone! Still only a marginally confident gardener, but with great aspirations (and a small yard), I encountered a few, ahem, challenges: Ledges and salt spray and fog, oh my. Snow storms and frost heaves and ice, oh my my!

That's when I joined a garden club—and you should too. While the dressy, oh-so-social atmosphere was a bit daunting at first, especially when I came to meetings directly from my oh-so-casual newspaper office at the

Boothbay Register, I met gardeners who really knew their stuff and were happy to share their secrets and stories. The monthly programs were a great way to learn what would grow in our area and where the best sources were. The tea sandwiches weren't bad either.

The formal atmosphere has lightened up a bit over the past dozen or so years. The meetings are more fun than in the "old days"—and the tea sandwiches and cookies are still delicious. I go whenever I can break away from work; and for programs that sound really good, I'll make even more of an effort.

It's become easier to justify going to the meetings since I joined the Coastal Maine Botanical Gardens' staff. As a reporter, I learned that the questions are as important as the answers. Even though I'm at CMBG to publicize Maine's first botanical garden, not to plant it, I have access to an endless roster of programs and am once again surrounded by horticulturists who can and will answer any gardening question with enthusiasm and accuracy.

But I've become a little weary of always having more questions than answers, which brings me to another step in this lifelong process of becoming the best gardener I can be in the least possible time. To cement what I'd picked up along the way—and to learn more, much more—I enrolled in the Master

Gardener program through the University of Maine's Cooperative Extension. As busy as you are, if you can make time to take the equivalent course in your area, I'd recommend it.

After 40 hours of class time and another 40 volunteer hours spread out over many months, additional hands-on workshops, fields trips and symposia, a second year of classes to fill in the gaps, and additional volunteer hours, I not only know some of the right questions to ask; I also feel comfortable being the one who answers them when people call for informa-tion. I have a huge notebook full of facts, and thanks to the 10-hour, take-home final exam, I know just where to find them.

Gardening is a lifelong pursuit. I'll continue to attend symposia and pro-grams, travel to remarkable public and private gardens both near and far, read everything I can find, and watch TV shows about gardening; and I recom-mend you do the same. Most impor-tantly, though, I'll take every possible moment to dig in my own ledge-filled, salt-sprayed, frost-heaved garden. It's mine, and I love it.

6

your gardening notebook— the most useful garden tool of all

Keeping a journal is only for people who have time on their hands, right? Not necessarily. Creating a personal gardening notebook that includes a journal can *save* you time, lots of time. It's the perfect tool for gardeners who can't stand to make the same mistakes twice and, on the other hand, love to repeat their successes. It makes beginners feel like they're in control of a pastime that can sometimes get the upper hand; for veterans, dog-eared garden notebooks are a beloved record of years spent digging in the dirt.

For a long time, I've known how important it is for a successful gardener to keep records, but I could never seem to manage it. With the best of intentions and lured by decorative covers and flower-strewn formats, I bought entire volumes of nearly blank pages with headings at the top and along the sides of each one. Some I received as gifts.

These journals-in-waiting assumed too much, though. Their focus was too narrow; there was no room to spread out, to think and muse, to scribble and doodle; there was no *flexibility*. That's why the pages stayed blank. Only after I devised my own, free-form notebook did it become easy and fun to keep track of what was happening in my garden.

Here's how you can make a notebook that will serve you well. It will always be a work in progress, and you can do as little or as much as you want, when you want.

GATHER YOUR SUPPLIES

I'll bet you already have a three-ring binder around the house. It doesn't have to be beautiful, not in the least. Here are some other items that will help you make the notebook your most useful tool of all: wide-ruled, three-hole paper; a few sheets of heavier paper (lined or unlined) on which you'll tape cards and seed packets; a package of index tab pages so you can organize your notebook into sections; a three-hole punch so you can add items other than notebook pages; clear tape; a three-ring zipper pouch along with a pencil, pens, a small ruler, and a good eraser to put in it. Colored pencils and pens or crayons can come in handy.

If the unbeautiful part bothers you, decorate the cover with adhesive paper or, easier by far, start with a pretty notebook. I use my kids' old school notebooks; by now, some of them have become rather retro.

Put an index tab page marked "Journal" at the very beginning. Insert a small pile of lined paper, and then add another index page, marking the tab "To Do" or "Tickler File." Add a dozen or so pages behind it. Add a few more index tabs, putting a few more sheets of paper behind each one. Name them according to your own whims or needs, or follow the suggestions below. If you write the tab headings in pencil initially, you can easily change them later. When you find out what works best for you, go over them in ink.

THIS NOTEBOOK IS GOLDEN

You've probably become accustomed to seeing, and maybe even tried using,

those neat little gardeners' diaries that have a space for jotting down your most intimate gardening thoughts, every single day, often leaving space for several years' jottings on each page. They can be beautiful, with tooled leather covers or charming botanical designs. Some even have cute little locks, and keys you can lose and then wonder about years later when they turn up under your socks.

These journals (or diaries) are a recipe for failure. The diarist's downfall is often the belief that he or she *must* write something every day. They're too much like fad diets: Skip one day, and you feel you might as well just give up.

Not so with your garden notebook! Wait till you actually think gardens, or talk gardens, or attend a garden club meeting or botanical garden program, or work in your garden or mess about with pots and shards in the garage. Then, as a reward for a job well done, even if it was only five minutes spent weeding on your way in from the car, or a minute spent learning about a good gardening manual or special tool, or hearing a new tip, or discovering a shortcut, jot down that information in your notebook.

When you want the information, it'll be right where you can find it. Of course, you could do the writing part on your computer. Somehow, though, it's more fun to use pen and paper. It's

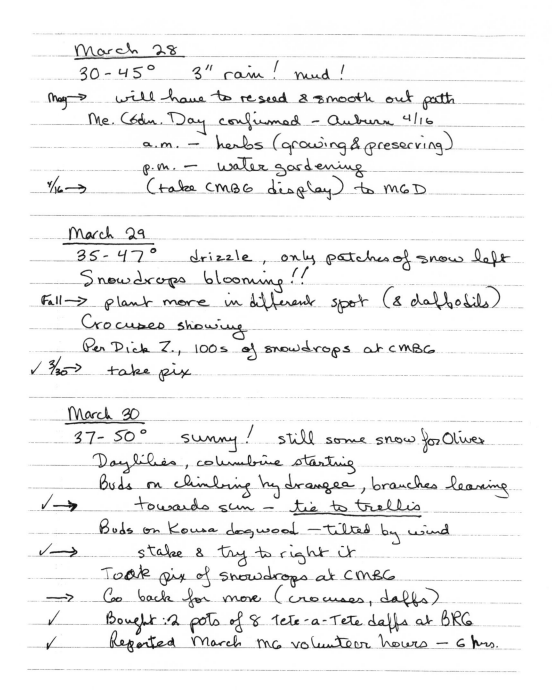

March 28
30-45°   3" rain! mud!
May → will have to reseed & smooth out path
       Me. Gdn. Day confirmed — Auburn 4/16
            a.m. — herbs (growing & preserving)
            p.m. — water gardening
4/16 → (take CMBG display) to MGD

March 29
35-47°   drizzle, only patches of snow left
       Snowdrops blooming!!
Fall → plant more in different spot (& daffodils)
       Crocuses showing
            Per Dick Z., 100s of snowdrops at CMBG
√ 3/30 → take pix

March 30
37-50°   sunny! still some snow for Oliver
       Daylilies, columbine starting
       Buds on climbing hydrangea, branches leaning
√ →   towards sun — tie to trellis
       Buds on Kousa dogwood — tilted by wind
√ →   stake & try to right it
       Took pix of snowdrops at CMBG
→   Go back for more (crocuses, daffs)
√   Bought: 2 pots of 8 Tete-a-Tete daffs at BRG
√   Reported March MG volunteer hours — 6 hrs.

a lot easier for most of us to do sketches that way, too; and you'll surely be moved to sketch. It's a way to illustrate your thoughts, to bring your ideas to life.

THE JOURNAL

Your garden journal will probably be the largest section of your notebook. Before long you'll develop a personal style, a special shorthand that speaks volumes. With that in mind, I'm going to offer you some tips and suggestions for what to include and ask you to take it from there. It's easy to get started and to keep going—all in your spare time.

- *Timing.* Don't worry if you don't begin recording in your new journal on New Year's Day. If it's January 1 and you're thinking green thoughts, fine; start now. If it's July 4, then start now instead. Whatever day it is when you're ready to begin, that's your starting point. Easy so far, right? It's about to get easier. When you're ready to record, open the notebook to the first section—your new garden journal. The top of Page One becomes Day One. At the end of the year, or if the book's full before then, start another book. The next year, start another. Make each a different color so you'll be able to tell them apart easily after you have a few years' worth collected. Label them on their spines for easier retrieval.

  Use your imagination, pick and choose as you please, and make additions according to your own style. Pretty soon you'll have a free-flowing record of your own gardening life—for better or for worse. And none of the space will be blank!

- *Date.* One thing I learned during years as a reporter is that you must always date your notes. That's just as true for gardeners. Without a date, much of what you write will become irrelevant. Just jot down the date at the top of each entry, and you can make useful comparisons. If you sow seeds and the resulting plants are spectacular—or if they fail miserably—when you planted them is an important part of the equation. Or if your memory's telling you that the daffodils that bloom every year should be popping up by now, you can check your journal to see if you're not just suffering from wishful thinking.
- *Sources.* Where did you hear the gardening tip, or buy the plant, or learn about the book? What's the title? What did it cost? What friends gave you cuttings from which gardens? Did they give you any pointers along with the plants? Keeping track of this kind of information can help jog your memory when you're trying to recall details from past seasons.
- *Current conditions.* What was the weather like today? Is there a trend? Just when you think it's never been this cold (or this hot), it's enlightening to look

back and see that there's nothing new under the sun. It was just this steamy (or just as cold) this time last year, and with even higher humidity (or snowfall).

- *Activities.* Did you shop for plants today? How'd it go? Did you plant a tree, or a row of seeds? How deep and far apart? Did you water? How and for how long? Or fertilize? What kind and how much? Did you move a plant into the sun or into the shade?

- *Reminders.* Is it almost time to prune the forsythia? Do you need to water that newly planted tree twice this week? Did you promise to divide some perennials for your neighbor? If the chore is coming right up in the next week or two, write it in today's notes in your journal and put an arrow or a circle next to it in the page margin. Using red or green ink will make it stand out even more. When you complete the task, put a check mark in the circle or across the arrow to indicate you've done it. Check back every few days to make sure you haven't missed any circles—and get a real sense of accomplishment from the check marks you can add. If you don't get around to a particular chore and have to postpone it (and this *will* happen), make a quick note under today's journal date referring you to the original date. Put a circle next to the new note. That way, the job won't get lost in the distant past. Small sticky notes or pointers on the edges of the pages act as good reminders, too. The important thing is to leave your notebook where you'll see it and use it.

- *Challenges and solutions.* What are you up against in your garden? How are the slugs this year? Did the beer or salt help? Did you use pesticides or herbicides? What were your soil test results? How many seedlings do you calculate it will take to fill this or that bed? Your journal is the place to keep track. Do a little math in the margins. Write down important phone numbers. Punch notebook holes in the letter with your soil test results and recommendations and insert it. Your notebook is all about being able to find what you need when you need it.

- *Dream on.* You want to plant a yellow magnolia or a dawn redwood next year? A thousand daffodils? You want to pull out that scraggly rose if it doesn't flower? Putting it in writing can plant the seeds of ideas that'll help your gardening dreams come true. Wishing *can* make it so.

MORE TABS HELP YOU KEEP TABS

Breaking your notebook into several parts will help you keep information at your fingertips. Use the index tab pages you've inserted after the "Journal" section to fine-tune your notebook.

- *"To Do."* There will be some tasks you won't be able to get to, or shouldn't get to, for some time: a couple of months, maybe a year—maybe even years. Create separate pages with the name of each month (and the current year) as a heading and add them to your notebook behind the index tab marked "To Do" or "Tickler File."

  As you're admiring your emerging bulbs in May and see that you need to fill in with more crocuses here or there, make a note on the October page to add *x* number of *x* bulbs. Draw a quick sketch to help you remember where you want to plant them. If you remember in August that you should have pruned back your forsythia just after it bloomed, put it on your page for the following May. Next year, you won't forget. Insert additional pages as needed. At the end of each month, consult the coming month's page to remind yourself what you decided way back when had to be done now.

- *"Plants."* You'll make notes about plants in the journal portion of your notebook, but there's a good reason to add a "Plants" index tab. If you start some of your garden from seed, cut the empty packets in half and tape them on a page in this section in such a way that you can turn them over to read the back. Do the same with plant tags or cultivation notes you make when friends give you plants from their own gardens. Heavier paper might be a good idea here to help support the packets and tags. Perhaps you want to insert an envelope and put them inside it; if so, be sure you can secure the flap so they don't fall out.

  Make separate pages with headings for favorite annuals, perennials, trees and shrubs, and bulbs; and put these in the "Plants" section, too. As you find plants in nurseries or see them in other gardens, add them to the appropriate pages. Leave room for future discoveries. If you think you'll be growing a lot of a particular variety, why not give this kind of plant its own page?

- *"Long-Range Projects."* As a reminder about projects or chores that are more than a year off, it's helpful to create a section marked "Long-Range Projects." When you think of future changes you'd like to make to your garden, jot them down on the pages in this section. Every so often, check out the ideas you've written just to see if (a) you've changed your mind; (b) it's still too soon; or (c) now is the time you can get them done.

- *"Resources."* You may already have your own favorite sources for plants and information, but you're bound to learn about more. Instead of amassing an untidy pile of business cards and scribbled notes and phone numbers, keep a section marked "Resources" where you can write in the information or tape in cards and notes. You might want to use heavier pieces of paper here, too, as a backing for notes; and make sure to tape only one edge if there's something on the back you'll want to read.
- *"Meeting Notes"* or *"Class Notes."* If you go to a garden club meeting or attend a horticulture class, why stick your notes or class handouts where you'll never find them again? This section is where you'll be able to look up that pruning technique you learned about last spring or the method for keeping amaryllis bulbs alive to bloom another

year. Remember to date your notes for future reference. When was that class again?
- *"Expenses."* Much as we hesitate to mention it, gardening costs money. Buying plants is just the beginning. There are the costs of fertilizer, mulch and compost, garden furnishings, pots and planters, and other living and nonliving elements of your garden. Then there are labor costs for any help you might hire, as well as indirect costs like water bills for keeping your garden growing. It's helpful to keep track of how much your landscaping efforts cost from year to year. Besides, 20 or 30 years from now, the figures will look quite reasonable, even quaint.

ILLUSTRATE YOUR IDEAS

Are plan and project details coming to mind? Keep a box of crayons, colored pencils, or color markers near your notebook, and start sketching. Even a plain old No. 2 pencil with an eraser is okay, but color is livelier and more fun.

Draw a planting diagram or a landscape plan. Rough in where thus-and-such bulbs are this year, and note where you want to add more in the fall. It's your book. You're allowed, and encouraged, to color outside the lines.

YOURS, ALL YOURS

The notebooks *you* create each year will be a much more useful tool than a prepackaged collection of pages that simply don't mesh with you or your gardening style. Don't be concerned if your current gardening interests and plans this year are entirely different in the future. In fact, it's very important—and lots of fun—to check back a year from now, and the year after that, to see what your notebooks have to tell you. *With luck, time, and effort, you will end up with both a garden you love and a collection of ragged, dirt-stained volumes that mean little to anyone else, but mean the world to you.*

7

growing by instinct

In many respects, gardening has a lot in common with the most important steps we take in our lives: raising children, acquiring pets, moving into a new house, beginning college, entering into a relationship or marriage, or starting a new job.

When we begin, we can never be entirely certain of what we're getting into. We're unaware of the exact nature of the pitfalls and rewards ahead, although we know there will surely be some. As time passes, we become more and more sure of ourselves until that aspect of our lives (parent, student, husband or wife . . . gardener) is part of who we are. The path becomes clearer. The mistakes we inevitably make, and the successes we achieve, are part of our personal learning curve and bring us closer to our goals, whatever they may be.

Of course, there's a great deal more at stake in raising a happy child, achieving a great marriage or a successful career, or graduating from school than there is in growing a gorgeous garden. Plants are easily replaced, and garden beds can be reshaped; it's harder with relationships and careers. Gardening is different, too, in that it's often a solitary activity, and we can often see dramatic and immediate results.

In all these endeavors, though, it's important for us to trust our instincts. We know more than we think we do, and in many cases more than others may think we do. Just get out in the garden and do what feels right. Make executive decisions. Take the life of a plant into your hands. You'll be amazed at what you can accomplish. If something you try doesn't work, you can try another plant or another technique until you get it right. It's great practice for *real* life.

8

what's your style?

Here's a chance for you to merge your personal style with your gardening style. Once you find yourself in the descriptions below, leave the stereotype behind. Sure, work within the time and abilities you have, but remember that preconceived notions of what you can and can't do are limiting. If you use the tips in following chapters to become more productive, you'll find yourself expanding self-imposed boundaries. You'll also have more time on your hands—time your hands could instead use for gardening.

GETTING TO KNOW YOUR INNER GARDENER

How do you feel about gardens and gardening, really? Take the following quiz to get in touch with the gardener you are and want to be.

1. My idea of a grand day at home is:
    (a) Hot-rodding around the yard on a riding mower
    (b) Sitting in the shade, feet propped up, with a cool drink and a tasty book
    (c) Romping with the kids
    (d) Organizing a good game of volleyball, badminton, or croquet (very "in" now)
    (e) Digging in the dirt, thinking of the flowers that will soon pop up and bloom
    (f) All of the above
2. My idea of gardening is:
    (a) Buying a pot of daisies or parsley at the supermarket and setting it on the windowsill, watering it when it begins to wilt
    (b) Mowing and fertilizing the lawn, and doing it all over again

(c) Planting bright annuals in containers and hanging pots and positioning them so they're visible and attractive

(d) Using a combination of containers and flower beds to brighten up my property

(e) Planting and tending bed after bed of flowers and other plants

(f) All of the above

3. My idea of a great garden is:

(a) A good view of my *neighbors'* perfect gardens

(b) One my friends and family and I can enjoy in many different ways

(c) Plantings in fantastic combinations of color and texture, size, and shape

(d) One that will give me the highest return on my time and money

(e) A beautiful space of which I can be proud

(f) All of the above

There are no right answers, except maybe (f) All of the above. You can have everything you want and need in a garden. It's all a matter of scale and degree, and it takes planning and time. The object is to create the best garden for you and leave you the time to enjoy it. Let's find out some more about you.

HOW DO YOU MANAGE TIME?

The way you use your time affects your gardening style. Do you fit into one or more of these time-eating categories? If so, you can use what you already know and are about to learn to jump-start your effectiveness in the garden. Who are you—really?

- *The Procrastinator.* Do you find yourself wondering in spring why you never planted those bulbs you bought last fall? Do you let flats of seedlings sit out all summer and pretend you meant them to be some sort of massed display? Do your children and pets get lost in the tall grass on your lawn? Keeping a garden notebook can help. It acts like a tickler file and, if you let it, will help you stay on top of your gardening chores (terrible word, *chores*). Just leaving the notebook in plain view in the house reminds you that there's a garden out there that needs your attention and affection.

- *The Perfectionist.* Do you fuss over one tiny part of your garden—or one plant—when everything else is going to seed, literally and figuratively? If something fails to thrive where you plant it, do you throw up your hands in disgust and throw it in the trash? Do you

the spare-time gardener

go ballistic if someone walks on your lawn, or if the kids' ball falls into a flower bed? Do you pull out plants that "volunteer," even if they're pretty? Once you go through the landscape planning process, you'll have a far better idea of the big picture. You'll know yourself and your garden a whole lot better and can plan according to what you've learned. You'll gain perspective—a very good thing in and out of the garden.

- *The Mad Scientist.* Do you use the shock-and-awe method of fertilization and weed control on your yard? Are you on a first-name basis with the exterminator? Do you frequent the pesticides aisle in the local garden center? Do you kill plants with kindness? Education will be your salvation. Follow the suggestions for learning about your garden and gardening. If you can adopt ecological gardening practices, you'll be on your way to saving time, money, and the environment.

- *The Good Neighbor.* Do you grow enough veggies to share with the entire neighborhood? Do people stop to take pictures of your garden and ask to purchase plants from you? Do you feel you need to cut your grass every weekend to the regulation length determined by surrounding lawns? All well and good, especially for the neighbors—unless you're secretly delivering monster zucchinis to them under cover of darkness! If all this magnanimity is wearing you out, though, you might want to back off a little. Grow what you need for yourself and your family—with a little left over for friends. Remember, when *your* vegetables are at their best, farm markets are selling *their* best, and cheaply. And that lawn! Once you know the alternatives, you might just hang up the key to your riding mower.

- *The Stress-Is-My-Middle-Name Worry-wart.* Are you edgy and full of angst? Do you fret a lot and pull out your hair over even the tiniest frustrations of everyday life? Do you come home from your job so exhausted that you only have energy to run the remote control? Get out in the garden. It'll do you good. You'll get fresh air and exercise that are healthy for the mind and body. Digging in the dirt relieves anxieties, and pulling weeds is a great way to rid yourself of tension. Soon you'll be humming and smiling.

The Parent of Small Children

Is exercise and fresh air an alien notion to your kids? Are they glued to the TV or video games whenever they're not in school or otherwise occupied?

Occupy them otherwise by making gardening a part of playtime. Set aside a small, sunny plot just for the kids; and edge it so it has distinct borders (this appeals to their territorial instincts). Choose plants that are dramatic and fast growing, and don't forget to add easy-to-grow edibles to the mix. It might be just the thing to convince them to eat their vegetables.

To start children in gardening so they'll be more likely to keep at it, go along with what they want. If they'd like to plant zucchinis, or pumpkins, or spaghetti squash, or cherry tomatoes, fine; make it happen. If they don't want to dig, let them rake instead. If they plant too many seeds in one place or water the garden with wild abandon, let them. Remember, they'll be your heart's delight long after the garden has faded. Besides, you can go back while they're not looking and tidy up after them—discreetly, please, so they don't think you're undermining their efforts.

THIS IS YOUR LIFE

Here are just a few of the roles in which you might find yourself—now and in the future. In just about any situation, you can come up with ways to grow something. And you should, because gardening is good for the soul; it beautifies our lives and helps us cope. Once you've found a personal fit in the descriptions below, garden accordingly. It will make the experience more fun and fulfilling *and* make you happier.

Starting plants from seed is a great way to introduce children to gardening. You can go all out and learn every detail of seed starting and growing; or, far better for our purposes (at least at first), go out and buy a couple of self-contained windowsill kits for growing seedlings. Then follow the instructions on the package carefully, and congratulate yourselves as seedlings emerge and the plants grow. On the day you transplant them to the garden, have a little celebration.

The Working Girl, or Guy (Outside of Home)

If you commute, does the daily trek require you to leave before dawn and return after dark—or does it only feel that way? When you get home, does peering at the yard while collapsing into a chair with a cold drink take all the energy you have? Does the idea of spending your weekends planting, weeding, or mowing send you into the slough of despair?

Plan for low maintenance and plant what looks good while you're around. White plants and pale or variegated foliage practically glow in the gloaming, even in the dark. Plant fewer but larger plants. Cover that ground with dense plantings and mulch heavily so weeds won't have a chance.

And don't forget to green up your work environment. A flowering plant or two at your desk, or wherever you spend the most time, will really brighten your day. Have a vase on hand and bring in a bunch of cut flowers, or send yourself a bouquet just to keep everyone guessing.

The Handyman or Handywoman

Do you buy every gardening gadget you see? Do you build and hang birdhouses and feeders? Have you installed gazebos and other structures throughout your yard? Do you try to do everything yourself, including limbing tall trees and hanging from scaffolding?

Good for you! But a little prudence in this department might save your neck. Know how to ask for help. Recognize that even if you *can* do everything, you might want to let someone else have the fun once in a while. As for those gadgets, do your homework so you won't waste time, space, and money on glitzy gizmos.

The Gourmet

Do you spend a fortune at your local fancy grocer's buying fresh herbs and organic vegetables? Do you insist on cooking with only the freshest ingredients?

Yum! When do we get to come over for dinner? In the meantime, why not let your plantings do double duty?

Make a kitchen garden; they're all the rage. Fill containers or garden beds with edibles rather than ornamentals, or a combination of the two. There's nothing like picking fresh vegetables from the garden; and, if you like, you can use organic growing techniques to keep everything as healthy and environment-friendly as possible.

Herbs come in a heady array of textures and colors, and snipping them for use in the stew only encourages them to grow bigger and better. If they're positioned below an open window or by a door, you'll have the bonus of marvelous scents wafting across the sill. In the winter, bring them into your kitchen. They'll be a source of fresh ingredients and provide a year-round display of greenery and fragrance.

The New Homeowner

Are you just starting out in your first home? Maybe you've downsized to a smaller home or even a condo.

Congratulations, and good luck in your new digs—literally. Plan a landscape that not only makes a splash right away in one small area, but that you can also sustain and expand upon in the future. No matter what the size, if you get the "bones" of your garden right the first time, you can fill in as time and money allow.

Take your time and live with what you have for a while before you decide

to change it. That way you'll see what's already planted and get to know your home and your site before making any decisions that might be difficult to reverse.

The Less Mobile Gardener

Do you have a hard time navigating or working in the garden, for whatever reason, but still want to enjoy gardening?

Choose perennials that require little care but look great from day one—and year after year. Save the annuals for containers or ready-made raised beds (all you add is soil), so you don't have to kneel as much, or maybe even at all.

WHERE DO YOU LIVE?
On a Large Property (over 1/2 acre)

Depending on just how big your property is, you may need help with the landscape design, planting, and continuing maintenance of your garden and land. However, the more you think about what you have already and what you want from a garden, and the more decisions and plans you make before you ever call in the pros, the easier and more economical it will be for you to create a beautiful, livable garden.

Unless you want people stopping to picnic in your backyard or teeing off on your lawn, thinking your property is a public park or golf course, you should stay away from objects, plants, and spaces that look too massive and commercial. On the other hand, if you have acres and acres of land, a cottage garden might not fit in with your home's look (then again, with planning and attention to scale, it could). If you separate your landscape into the rooms that accommodate your outdoor living needs, and then make sure they're connected in a graceful, practical way, the space will come together for you.

On a Small Property (1/2 acre or less)

Congratulate yourself for all the time you've saved. You can still have a great garden, as long as you keep it in scale with your house. For the same reason you probably wouldn't bring home an Irish wolfhound, you shouldn't plant a spreading, 30-foot-tall shrub, much as you might dearly love them both.

You'll do best by combining and layering uses in your outdoor living spaces—putting the play area where you relax after the kids have gone to bed, the barbeque where you have your morning coffee, a potting table where you keep the hose. You get the idea.

Planting containers with vegetables among, or instead of, ornamentals keeps you in fresh produce, and it greens up the yard, too. Using dwarf shrubs and trees postpones the need for pruning.

It's always a good idea to check out the other gardens in your immediate neighborhood; you'll learn what thrives in your area and what the overall style is. Of course, that isn't to say you can't do something totally different with yours. Just be aware that you might get a little flak from the people next door.

In an Apartment or Condo

Are your gardening options limited to a tiny yard or a balcony? Or is a windowsill the only place you can exercise your green thumb? Does someone else own the building? If so, it's understandable if you don't want to invest a fortune in plants or structures for the garden. Do you own a condo? Contractors probably take care of the overall maintenance, but you may be left with a postage-stamp-sized space in which to try out your garden skills.

No matter; you can create a striking display. Use containers and more containers, choosing different sizes. They should be in scale with the size of the area, rather than overwhelming the space, and they should leave you room for a table and chairs, a hibachi, or whatever you need to make your outdoor area your own. Or use window boxes (suspended inwards on the railing if they might otherwise crash down upon unsuspecting passersby). If you have a little chunk of land, you can add some ground covers and an ornamental tree and a shrub or two, depending on the size of the garden.

Whatever containers you select, fill them with plants that fit the light conditions you can give them. You might be able to leave them right in the pots they came in and arrange those in the containers, covering it all with mulch or moss for a pulled-together look.

If you have a sunny spot, why not try veggies in containers, too? You can buy them already in bud, and having even one plant's worth of plump, ripe tomatoes at your beck and call can raise your culinary efforts to new levels. Besides, they make gorgeous, if perishable, decorative objects. Herbs and lettuces are terrific container plants, and they look and taste wonderful.

If the great outdoors is inaccessible at this stage of your life, grow houseplants with wild abandon. Create a lush indoor garden. The plants will freshen the inside air you breathe—and your outlook.

part two

Getting to Know Your Garden

9

not so fast!

Okay, so your little (or big) plot is never going to rival Louis XIV's Versailles (remember, Marie Antoinette lost her head both in and out of the garden). You might not grow prize-winning blooms or state-of-the-art vegetables. Cars may not screech to a halt to marvel at your home's curb appeal.

But your garden can be beautiful and welcoming, a relaxing and colorful place where you can spend time in green surroundings and grow enough flowers to brighten your life and enough fresh veggies to add taste to your table. You can have fun there, too, and even stop and smell the roses (if you choose to grow them); and you won't have to devote every spare moment to its upkeep or hire a crew of professionals.

The catch? You have to put in some thought; and yes, a little money, too. You need to get and stay organized.

There are plenty of ways to save time, and money, and still have a garden where you'll enjoy working and living. Your garden is an extension of your home; and your life will be richer if you love your outdoor living space as much as, or even more than, the indoor rooms.

IN THE BEGINNING

There's an expression: Begin as you mean to go on. In the garden, you should begin with a plan—a practical and practicable plan. Before you touch a trowel or handle a hoe, you must think! You must ask yourself a lot of questions, first about the area where you garden, then about the way you want to use your land, and finally about what you want to plant. Throughout the process, you should consider the amount of time you're willing and able to put into gardening.

Doing these exercises up front will save you a lot of time, effort, and cash later on. It's also an exercise in patience, since what you really want to do is surround yourself with glossy catalogues (if it's winter) and order everything that appeals to you or (if it's spring or summer) spend hours at the local garden center and come home with a carload of bloomin' plants. But resist the urge and instead gather the paper, pencils, and other supplies listed; find a comfy spot; and take the first step towards spare-time gardening.

THE WAIT-AND-SEE APPROACH— A PROCRASTINATOR'S DREAM

Speaking of patience, the best way to assess what your landscape has to offer is to wait an entire year before making any major landscaping or gardening decisions. This is particularly true if you're new to your home.

In the meantime, you can always put up hanging baskets, fill window boxes to overflowing, and dot container gardens around your property— all easily done. Leave digging in the dirt till later. By then you'll have a much better idea of what you already have and what you want, and you can proceed with more confidence.

If you've lived in one place for at least a year, you should have a pretty good idea of what's in your yard. It still doesn't hurt to wait and see—taking notes all the while. How's that for a legitimate rationalization?

While you're waiting—and certainly before you fill out those order forms or pull a wagon full of plants up to the garden center's cash register—take the time to look at and complete the exercises in upcoming chapters.

10

help!

There are a whole lot of people out there who know a whole lot about gardening. In spite of what they may tell you—or what you might fear—not one of them was born with a green thumb. Their ability to tell weed from flower was not innate, their desire to speak botanical Latin not inborn, their sense of landscape design definitively not learned in the cradle. Gardening may be part intuition and part blind luck, but it's mostly an acquired skill.

So, how have all these people gotten to know so much about gardening? Well, it began with an interest—and *you* already have that. They pursued their interest—and *you* can do that. And then, if they liked the results of their efforts, they went out of their way to learn even more—and *you* certainly can, too.

YOUR NEW BEST FRIENDS

Did you know there are plenty of people just hankering to help you with your garden? They want to get you off on the right foot and then keep you enthusiastic and committed to what for some is a favorite pastime, and for others is an abiding passion.

Sure, there's something in it for them, but often it's just the satisfaction they get from sharing their own expertise and love of gardening. And if it's money they want, you can get a lot of value for a well-considered dollar.

"Who are these people," you ask, "and where can I find them?" They're all around you.

Visit Your Local Nursery

If you want to know what grows well in your area, or what grows too much and too fast, hang out at your local nursery. It's worth a visit simply to be surrounded by the scents, colors, and textures that will bombard your senses. Keep your eyes open, read signs and plant tags, and ask lots of questions. Don't be shy; the people who work there spend years learning their trade, and it's their job to help you. They keep up with all the latest advancements, both in plants and ways to grow them, and they're usually happy to help bring you up to speed. Since it's way too easy to be overwhelmed by the array of plants around you, take a small notebook. As you walk around, jot down any questions that spring to mind. In fact, you'll probably come up with some before you ever leave home.

Of course, it's best to choose your time wisely. If you go at 9 a.m. on a gorgeous Saturday morning in spring when the garden center is packed with customers, the staff will barely have time to say that'll be $76.99 please, let alone tell you what will do best in that dry, shady spot beside the back door. However, if the nursery's busiest time is the only time you can get there, well, it'll just have to do.

You should try to resist the urge to make impulse purchases until after you've created your landscape and planting plans. Then we'll go shopping in earnest. Don't buy anything unless you know where you're going to put it and why, how big it's going to get, and what kind of tender loving care it's going to need from you. I know, I know; that glorious rose bush would look great in your yard; but think first, then buy.

Discover Your Local Cooperative Extension Office

These go by different names—agricultural or university extension, cooperative extension, county agent, and on and on. Whatever the name, chances are there is one somewhere in your county or state. These people are my heroes. They know everything about plants and the problems that beset them, and they spend their days happily solving people's gardening problems—usually for free. Just look them up in your phone book and give them a call (if you can't find a phone number, check with the horticulture department at your nearest college, or go online).

You can send the extension service a soil sample in the kit they'll provide, and you'll get back a detailed profile of your soil and how to grow whatever takes your fancy. You can send or take them pieces of nasty-looking diseased or infested plants, and you'll make their day—plus you'll find out what's wrong and how to fix it.

Attend "Garden Day" or an Agricultural Fair

To really immerse yourself, attend your version of what in our state is called "Maine Garden Day." It's a whirlwind day full of slide lectures and how-to classes on a multitude of subjects—everything from tackling pesky insects to creating beautiful arrangements (flowers provided!), from planting in shade or containers to building your own, personal labyrinth. If you join the hundreds who attend, I guarantee you'll come away newly energized about gardening and ready to apply all you've learned. To find a garden day in your state, contact the agricultural extension service or local university.

Agricultural fairs are great fun and can be educational for the entire family. You'll see an amazing array of creatures, tools, arts and crafts, products, and regional culinary delights. The Common Ground Fair and Blueberry Day at other fairs are our favorites.

Meet the Master Gardeners

Trained through the above extension services, these enthusiastic gardeners live to share what they've learned through many hours of classroom work and as many or more hours of volunteer time. If you have a question, there's a good chance that a master gardener can answer it—or find the answer for you.

Some of these men and women develop enough expertise and experience that they present a wide variety of programs through botanical gardens and arboreta, adult education programs, nonprofit farms, and growers' groups. They offer some of the classes at garden days.

Master gardeners put in volunteer time creating plantings at historic sites and buildings, hospitals, and properties owned by nonprofit organizations and government entities. In Maine, every Monday throughout the summer a reliable and devoted group travels by lobster boat to a state-owned island to plant and tend '50s-style gardens around a lighthouse. It's part of a living museum project, and it's a great gig.

But I digress. Find a master gardener through the extension offices or classes, and you've opened an avenue to lots of information. Better yet—take the course!

Join the Club

Garden clubs come in all sizes and shapes; and chances are there's one that's perfect for you. At their best, they can offer good times with other people who enjoy gardens and gardening; opportunities to volunteer (if you have the time); and programs, classes, and workshops to increase your knowledge and hone your gardening skills.

You can attend the meetings and workshops that suit you and opt out when the subject isn't on your personal gardening agenda. You might want to join the program committee; then you could suggest the speakers and workshops that appeal the most to you. And if you'd like to hear them, chances are your fellow club members would too.

It shouldn't be hard to find a garden club if there's one nearby. Look for notices in the local newspaper, or ask at a garden center. If there is no club, you might consider getting together with like-minded friends and starting your own—in an informal sort of way.

Go for the Gardens

Public gardens, that is. There are botanical gardens all over the world, and you can learn something from each and every one of them. They're tucked into cities and spread out over rural landscapes. They're in the tropics and on alpine meadows—and everywhere in between. Depending on the facility, you'll find a wide range of styles, from giant glass conservatories and historic buildings to wooded paths and sprawling cottage gardens.

There is an equally wide variety in the amenities that await you, from vending machines for sodas and snacks to museum-quality shops and gourmet restaurants. There are imaginative gardens and activities specifically for children and many programs for adults.

And don't forget arboreta. An arboretum is a garden that concentrates primarily on its collection of trees, rather than on floral displays, although many arboreta have gorgeous flowers, too.

At public gardens and arboreta, you can soak up the verdant atmosphere and absorb a great deal of information just by seeing the selections, and where and how they're planted and tended. And, of course, these wonderful resources are where you can find experts (volunteers and staff) who are willing and able to answer just about any question you can toss their way.

Next time you take a vacation, check out the travel guides for public gardens you can visit along your route or at your destination. They offer a window into the *nature* of a place—literally.

Take a Tour

One thing pretty much all nonprofit organizations have in common is the need to bring in money. They count on donors, but they also rely on special fund-raising events. One of the most popular types of fund-raisers is the garden tour, or house and garden tour, or kitchen tour. These, too, run the gamut from visits to a single house and/or garden to megatours of a half-dozen or so magnificent homes and the gardens surrounding them. Find the time to go on as many of these as you can, no matter what the type and size. You'll learn something, and you'll have a great time.

SPEND TIME TO MAKE TIME

All of the above ways to learn more about gardening should also give you insight into how you want to spend your gardening currency—time *and* money. They'll help you decide what's important to you and, conversely, what might be more than you want to tackle. Or, you might try a small-scale version of some grander gardening effort—an herb garden patterned after an historic knot garden, say, or a grouping of interesting containers on your deck or porch (or apartment balcony) instead of one lonely window box or potted geranium.

Your garden should reflect *your* vision of *your* home landscape. It's for your enjoyment, and the more you learn, the closer you can come to achieving the goal of a garden that suits you—and the time you have to spend on it.

II

easy ways to a "perfect" garden

Call me a perfectionist. It's okay; but I think of myself as an "imperfect perfectionist." I really like everything to look just right, perfect—neat and clean and well groomed; and that goes for the garden, too. But, alas, I'm so very far from actually *being* perfect, and so is the world immediately around me, that achieving perfection is way out of reach. In fact, it's impossible for you, for me, for everyone. What to do, what to do?

Take heart. There are tricks of the trade, sleight of hand if you will, to at least make your garden consistently look neat and clean and well groomed, even if isn't all those things. It's possible to create the illusion without spending all your time, or all your money having someone else do the work. Here are some ideas for splicing garden chores into your week as painlessly as possible:

- Keep a large basket with a handle (a trug or market basket) or a very portable trash basket near the door, and take it along whenever you take a stroll in the garden to admire your very own slice of nature. If you see a small stick that's fallen, pick it up then and there and stow it in the basket or bag (bigger sticks have to go in an out-of-the-way pile); if you see flowers that need deadheading, pick off as many as you can in one minute (you don't have to get every single one) and put them in there too. It's having the container at your side that makes all the difference.

Once a week, spend a little more time and do a more thorough job. Of course, you won't have nearly as much to do because of your piecemeal pickups throughout the week. Put all of what you collect in a pile out of sight, and when the pile is big enough, or you're making a dump run anyway, take it all to your local recycling facility.

- By doing a quick cleanup every time you go out in the garden you accomplish two things: The garden consistently looks better than it otherwise would, and giant cleanups that seem to take forever will pretty much be a thing of the past.

- Buy lawn furniture and ornaments with durability in mind. If it's going to need painting every spring, let some other customer have that pleasure. If it's in a color that will show every speck of dust, find another color. The furniture you add to your landscape should be serviceable and in scale with you and your surroundings. If you like to serve a meal for four or six, or spread out the morning paper as you enjoy your cup of coffee on the patio, then don't purchase a spindly bistro dining set with a tiny table and delicate chairs. Find a sturdy dining table and seating, or combine pieces that coordinate well to create your own look. If children will be using your garden, why not invest in a kid-sized picnic set? They

withstand anything, clean up easily, and let your youngsters feel included.

- Unless you're a super handyman or handywoman, building a playhouse or tree house can be a time-consuming project. You might be better off purchasing one ready-made. Some swing sets come with their own canopied "tree" house at one end.

- Speaking of dust, figure out the color of the dust you and the wind stir up in your yard. In some areas, the soil is tan; in others it's gray or red, or even white. Try to choose your decking and flooring with that in mind. For instance, if the dust you find in your house is predominately tan, avoid gray decking or flooring. If it's gray, avoid tan. If you use a color that blends in with the soil, you'll have to sweep and clean less often; and your outdoor living areas will look better between sweepings.

- Do as much as possible to put your garden to bed in the fall, when there are fewer distractions. Cut back and remove tall stalks and other plant debris. That way, come spring you won't be cleaning up last year's mess when you really want to be planting and growing. It will also make your garden look neater all winter.

That's important because even when it lies dormant, your landscape is part of the overall impression your home gives.

• When you're raking in the fall, you should clear off the lawn, but leave a layer of leaves on the garden. Once the ground has frozen, cover the leaves with a couple of inches of mulch to further protect the plants. When spring arrives and the soil is workable, dig the nicely aged mulch and leaves into the ground to enrich it. You now have a blank canvas onto which you can "paint" your new plants.

• Filling your space with larger patches or swaths of a few plants does more than create a more pleasing effect than using just one or two each of many different plants to fill the same area; it also saves time. It's easier to select, purchase, haul, and work with large flats of one kind of seedling than with a six-pack of this and another of that and yet another of something else. If you want more variety than this approach offers, why not purchase flats of a multicolored species? You'll still have the continuity of having one kind of plant throughout a particular area, and you'll have a range of colors that naturally complement each other well.

• Once you've decided which plants you want, and have considered their ultimate size in your landscape plan, purchase the biggest specimens you can find and afford. You'll be that much closer to a mature garden that looks like it belongs in its space.

• As a friend told me by way of spring and summer garden advice, "Mulch, mulch, mulch." That says it all, and it can't be said often enough. Deep brown (not orange, please) mulch sets off a garden beautifully, keeps weeds from growing and makes them easier to pull out if they do, retains moisture, adds nutrients to the soil (especially if the mulch is nicely aged), and improves the soil's texture. As soon as you've planted and watered a garden area, spread a couple of inches of finely shredded mulch around the plants, keeping it slightly away from the stems if possible, and rake it fairly smooth. You'll like what you see.

You can get away with the larger-textured bark mulch in areas where plants such as shrubs are big and sturdy, but a finer mulch is easier to handle in an ornamental garden of annuals or perennials. Some people like cocoa bark mulch (though it's toxic to dogs) and say it smells like chocolate. It's fun to work with but is also very light, so you have to be careful it doesn't blow around when it's dry. As for the chocolate smell, take it from a chocoholic: It's a long way from "best dark."

12

the lay of the land—exercise 1

Without any soul searching at all, you've already planned and planted one 32-square-foot garden. Now the time has come to search your gardener's soul. In the process, you'll become aware of your property in a new way and learn a little about yourself, too.

The exercises below may sound complicated as you're first reading about them. Follow the directions, one step after another, and you'll soon find that they're actually quite simple, enlightening, and even fun.

If you can't spare the time right now, go through the steps and questions and then start with just one section of your property. When there's more time, you can do more. Since success breeds success, once you get some gardening under your belt and see the results, you'll *want* to get out there more and more.

GETTING STARTED

First, surround yourself with your supplies. Improvise if you don't have those listed below:

- *Supplies for Step One*—a notebook or clipboard with paper (if it has grid lines on it, all the better), a 25- or 50-foot measuring tape, a pencil and good eraser, a magnetic compass if you have one (the kind for telling directions, not for making circles), and a tote bag or box so you can keep everything handy. If you don't have a compass, you surely know where the sun comes up and sets, so simply note those as east and west; you'll be close enough.
- *Supplies for Step Two*—a pad (or roll) of large tracing paper (11-by-17-inch or 18-by-24-inch sheets), several sheets of ledger-size

paper (11 by 17 inches, with grid lines if available), a smooth desktop or table, quick-release masking tape or large paper clips to secure papers to the backing, your pencil and good eraser, and the box or bag to hold it all. Here too, colored pencils are helpful and add a festive feel to what you're doing.

- *Supplies for Subsequent Steps*—same as above.

STEP ONE

The object of this exercise is to record the lay of the land and remind yourself of what you have on it. Choose a fine, sunny day with little or no wind. With notebook or clipboard in hand, walk your property, taking and recording measurements (a friend or family member is an asset here), check your compass orientation (or judge by the sun if you don't have a compass handy), and make a very rough sketch.

While you're making this working sketch, note on it the placement of buildings (with doors and windows), streets, large trees, ledges or boulders, fences, and other more or less permanent objects.

If you have or can get a plat plan or survey from your town office, it can help you as you make your base drawing. Grid paper will make the drawing process easier, too. Your sketch doesn't

have to be accurate to the inch. It's a tool—and a beginning.

STEP TWO

Now, back inside, redraw your initial sketch onto a ledger-size piece of paper, being a bit neater this time and trying to draw to scale (1 inch = 10 feet, for example). The larger size is easier on the eyes and enables you to be more accurate. Again, grid lines help but aren't essential.

Sketch in a rudimentary compass rose to give you a sense of which parts of your garden are sunny. Using whatever shorthand or squiggles work for you, add the stationary objects you noted before. If your property is too large to do this easily on one sheet of paper, divide and conquer using different sheets for different sections of the land or different garden areas.

This is not a fine-art assignment. The drawing can be "draft-y" and doesn't need to be exact; but, as with your initial notes, it shouldn't be too far off. What's most important is that you're getting a better feel for the area where you garden and for your property as a whole. You've just created your base drawing.

Draw dark reference lines just in from the corners of the paper so you can match up this drawing with others on the tracing paper that will go over it. To give yourself some flexibility to make

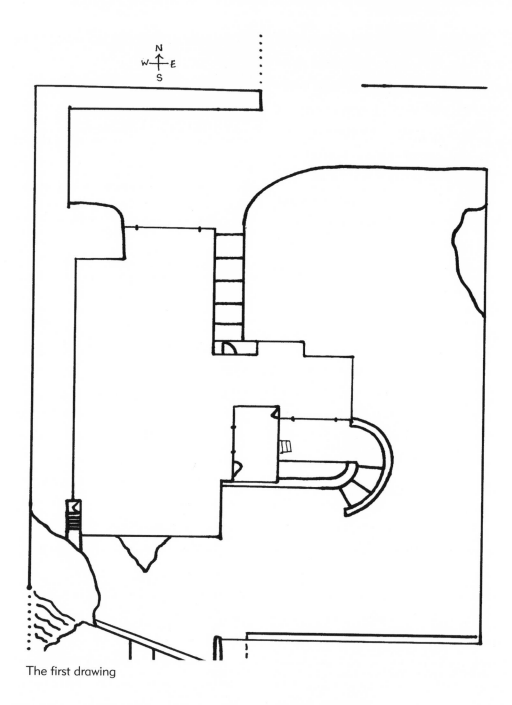

The first drawing

changes without going back to the drawing board, literally, it's a good idea to have a copy shop run off several ledger-size prints as backup.

Attach this page to your desk or table with the low-adhesive masking tape, which won't mar the surface.

STEP THREE

Here's another excuse to get some fresh air. Take a look at the long list of outdoor conditions below, and then go back outside with this book and make notes next to the ones that apply to your property.

the spare-time gardener

Alternatively, you can take a copy of your base drawing outside and make notes on that, although its size might make it unwieldy.

OUTDOOR CONDITIONS

Slopes (steep or slight?) _____

_____

Damp areas and drainage _____

_____

High and dry spots _____

_____

Areas that are perpetually shady _____

_____

Areas where there's partial shade for

most of the day _____

_____

Spots where it's sunny six or more

hours per day _____

_____

The location of faucets _____

_____

The drip line from the roof _____

_____

The direction of prevailing winds (these

can change from season to season) _____

_____

The trunks of deciduous trees and the

area covered by branches and leaves ____

_____

_____

Areas covered by evergreens _____

_____

Other plantings that you like and want

to keep _____

_____

Plants and trees you don't want to keep

_____

Plants that aren't thriving where they are but that you don't want to toss _____

_____

Paths and walkways that you like and want to keep _____

_____

Other hardscape that you don't want to move (patios, swing sets, gazebos, etc.)

_____

Ponds and pools _____

_____

Septic system _____

_____

Roads and driveways _____

_____

Streetlights _____

_____

Fireplugs _____

_____

Great views (from which floor or floors?) _____

_____

Crummy views (from which floor or floors?) _____

_____

Other conditions that apply _____

_____

_____

_____

STEP FOUR

Place a piece of tracing paper over your drawing, and secure it with more tape or the clips. If it's larger than the drawing, you can wrap it over the edges if necessary and then attach it. Trace the reference lines from your base drawing onto this sheet to help keep everything aligned.

Guided by your notes and your memory, indicate on the tracing paper over your base drawing the location of any of the above conditions that apply to your property. Again, use your own shorthand—lines, arrows, words, circles, or whatever personal system makes sense to you. Remember to keep the reference lines aligned as you draw.

Just by going through this exercise, you'll have already noticed that some of these elements are things you definitely want to have in your garden and see from your home, while there are others you'd rather were camouflaged or hidden. Some are moveable or removable, some aren't. You have absolutely no control over some; others are entirely yours to do with as you please.

You've just taken a giant step towards a landscape plan that you can use for many purposes and for years to come.

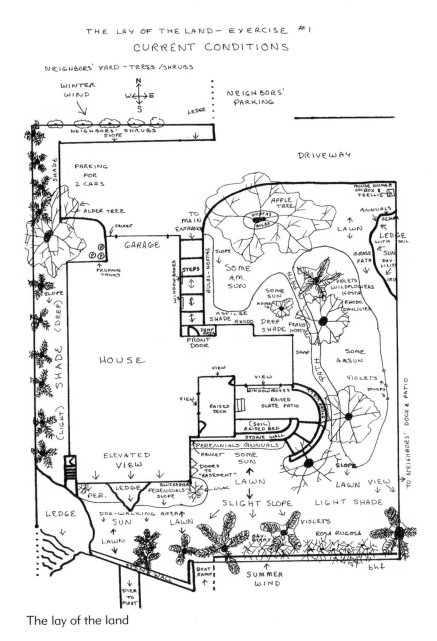

The lay of the land

13

just imagine— exercise 2

Put all these supplies away for the moment and head outside again. Just look around you for a minute or two, and then close your eyes and simply picture how you want to use your garden in the coming season or the next year or two. Now imagine how you might want to use it five or ten years into the future. Feel free to dream large (but don't fall asleep at this juncture; there's more).

To help your imagination along, ask yourself the following questions, and any others that come to mind. Jot down the answers for future reference. One thing's for certain, though: Whatever you imagine now will be different from what you have in mind a year from now—or five or ten years from now. Relax; this is only an exercise. It's meant to be helpful, not stressful. Gardening is a fluid concept.

THIS IS YOUR OUTDOOR SPACE: HOW DO YOU WANT TO USE IT?

Do I want to entertain outdoors? _____

_____

If so, is my style casual or formal? _____

_____

What's the maximum number of people

likely to be in the yard at one time?

What's the usual number of people

who'll be there? _____

_____

_____

Do I want to barbeque? If so, to what extent—a tiny hibachi or a massive, propane-powered outdoor cooking extravaganza? _____

_____

How do I want to use my landscape in winter? Will the kids be building snow forts and snowmen, flooding a small place to ice skate, sledding if there's room and any size hill? _____

_____

_____

In warmer weather, what will we do outside—play games, frolic in the pool, sit in the shade and read books, catch some rays, all of the above and then some? _____

_____

_____

If I need a place where children or adults can play in warm weather, should these be hard or soft surfaces? A marked-off court? How much space will the games or activities take up. Are we talking about baseball or tennis here, or simply a place to put a wading pool, toss a basketball at a hoop, or practice soccer kicks into a net? _____

_____

_____

Do I need a place where my dog(s) can run? Or be confined? Do my cats go outside? _____

_____

Which entrance to my house do I use most frequently? Do I want to change that? _____

_____

Which entrance do I want guests to use?

_____

Do I need a sheltered spot for parcel

and/or mail delivery? _____

_____

Do I need a signpost for my house

number, or will it go on the mailbox or

the side of the house? _____

_____

Is there a place everyone walks (neigh-

bors on their way to visit, kids on their

way to and from school, delivery peo-

ple) where the lawn or flowers simply

won't grow? _____

_____

Do I want a private outdoor nook for

myself? For someone else in my family?

If so, where do I want it to be? _____

_____

Or do I need a building (workshop,

studio, storage shed, playhouse)? _____

_____

If so, what size and style would I like it be?

_____

Where will I mess about with plants and

soil? _____

_____

Where and how will I store my tools and

supplies? _____

_____

WHAT ELSE DO YOU NEED TO CONSIDER?

Am I happy with the amount of shade/

sun in my yard? If not, how much more

(or less) do I want or need? _____

_____

Where are the best views? The worst? __

_____

What do I want to hide (air condition-

ers, propane tanks, trash cans, etc.)? __

_____

What pests do I need to control—

mosquitoes, Japanese beetles, aphids?

_____

_____

Are there other unwelcome visitors to

my yard—deer, raccoons, snakes? _____

_____

What wildlife do I want to encourage—

ladybugs, earthworms, bats, birds? _____

_____

Can I get water to every part of my

property? _____

_____

Do I live where there are ever, or often,

water shortages or droughts? _____

And . . . What else comes to mind

for my particular spot? _____

_____

WHAT ARE YOUR WORRIES AND CONCERNS?

No matter where you live, it's important to think of safety—for yourself and for your children, other people's children, neighbors, and pets . . . even those who are uninvited. This isn't merely a question of liability; it's a moral and emotional issue. Just think how you'd feel if someone were hurt. You have an obligation to make your property as safe as possible for you and others.

As you ask yourself these questions, they may trigger thoughts of other potential problems. That's okay. In fact, it's probably a good idea to consider worst-case scenarios, as long as we don't make ourselves worry to an inordinate degree. Caution is fine, but we get no points for being obsessive.

Am I concerned about traffic—either

because children will be playing in the

yard or because it's dangerous pulling

out of my driveway? _____

_____

If I have a pond or pool, even a tiny fishpond or wading pool, is it 100 percent safe for people and pets? _____

_____

Is security an issue? Are there easy hiding places around my house? _____

_____

_____

What else is on my mind? _____

_____

How do I feel about privacy? _____

_____

Am I territorial? _____

_____

Do I like and trust my neighbors? _____

_____

Do I want or need a fence around my property, my pool, my garden? _____

_____

WHAT YOU ALREADY GROW VS. WHAT YOU WANT TO GROW

Do I have a lawn? Do I want a lawn? If so, how big should it be? _____

_____

_____

Do I have a compulsive need to have grass Tiger Woods would recognize from golf greens he has known? _____

_____

Would I be willing to substitute ground cover or flower beds for some or all of the grass? How much of the lawn can I convert to other uses? _____

_____

_____

Do those "instant and carefree" wildflower meadows appeal to me? _____

_____

Do I want to grow flowers? If so, do I have a preference—annuals, perennials, evergreens, or a mixture? _____

_____

Are there any plants I particularly like? Where did I see them? Where can I get them? _____

_____

_____

_____

Do I want to cut flowers for arrangements? _____

_____

Do I want to grow vegetables? Herbs? Fruit? _____

_____

If so, what are my preferences? _____

_____

_____

_____

Do I have a pathological need to have the first (or biggest, or reddest) tomato on the block? _____

_____

Does my garden have a focal point? If not, do I have one in mind? _____

_____

How's my soil? Have I had it tested? ___

_____

What do my nearest and dearest like and want to see in the garden? In the yard? _____

_____

Somewhere in this process, ask family members and others who'll be spending a lot of time in your newly revitalized garden if they have any favorite plants. Or any they detest. My mother particularly loved peonies and lily of the valley but, for some reason, couldn't stand hollyhocks. Since she visited often and liked spending time in the garden, I always kept her preferences in mind when planting. Then we moved into a house that sported glorious hollyhocks in its garden, as well as her beloved peonies and lily of the valley. She thought they were *all* lovely, so they *all* stayed put. The lesson is: When possible, try to please everyone. A garden should never be a battleground—especially since you'll be calling on these same people to help with the watering and weeding.

14

money matters—exercise 3

Now that you've pictured your garden in all its glory, it's time to take a sobering look at your budget and your bank account. Ask yourself how you want to spend the money available to you for landscaping and gardening.

When selecting plants, remember that perennials give you value year after year. Annuals may brighten the garden for only one season, but they do so as very few perennials can.

Add to the money mix what you are able to spend on containers and/or window boxes, compost, brackets, gnomes, what have you. Depending on what you have in mind, the cost of these items can be astronomical; but there are real bargains to be had—especially at end-of-season sales, auctions, yard sales, flea markets, and the like. Just be sure before you buy a "bargain" that it has staying power, both in durability and in suiting your tastes. Gnomes (or pink flamin-

goes, or gazing balls) may be back in style, but for how long? And how long will it be before you get a little tired of that flash of red concrete or pink plastic every time you look at your garden?

Further, consider whether you want or need to include major projects in your garden. Do you want to purchase a fence? Do you need to regrade your property to improve drainage? Are you ready to add a swimming pool? A stone patio or deck? If so, get more than one estimate if possible, and hire the best professionals you can find and afford.

Once you know what you want and need, ask yourself the following questions:

How much do I want to spend each season on plants and landscaping? _____

_____

Will that change anytime soon, or will it stay fairly steady from year to year? _____

_____

Do I need to purchase tools and equipment? How much will they cost? _____

_____

What kind of ornaments and structures do I want to buy? How much will they cost? _____

_____

Is it worth it to me to hire professionals to come in and help? _____

_____

If so, what level of expertise do I need?

_____

If not, how much time and toil am I willing to spend? _____

_____

Can I afford major projects now? Do I want to do everything at once or in phases? _____

_____

What other expenses do I need to include in my gardening/landscaping budget? _____

_____

_____

_____

15

lawn vs. garden—
and the winner is . . .

You've worked out how much of your yard you need to devote to activities—fun and games, barbequing, play area, etc. Now please stop there. These days, most of us have more lawn than we need, and on a regular basis we smother a lot of it in pesticides, herbicides, and fertilizers. We water and water it to achieve just the right shade of emerald green.

Then we mow it, and hardly any of us do that with sweat equity and a push mower anymore. It's fossil fuels we're using to make that lawn into an ersatz putting green, like the rest of the yards in the neighborhood. And the noise! Have you been to a suburban neighborhood on a summer Saturday? The drone of the riding mowers is deafening.

If you have sun, and do all the "right" things, your grass will grow . . . and grow . . . and grow. It's

unfortunate that we spend so much time helping grass thrive, only to mow it down in its prime. Except in areas where you want the greensward for outdoor living, what indeed is the point?

Okay, okay, I'm a lawn curmudgeon . . . and you should be one too.

I'd urge you to determine the minimum amount of lawn you need, and then turn under the rest of that grass and use the space for something else. But what else?

There are a lot of alternatives. You can create flower beds or a woodland garden, or you can plant ground covers. Pavers, gravel, and decking are the best choice for some areas, and container gardens can add color and life to these surfaces. Doesn't that sound more interesting than plain old grass?

LOVE THE LAWN YOU KEEP

In spite of all our best intentions, most of us have some lawn. We feel we need it to connect different areas in the yard and to provide outdoor play and living space, and also because a yard wouldn't be a yard without grass, right? So, if we're going to have some lawn, how do we make the best of it?

- Between mowings, let it grow just a little longer and don't take off as much as you think you should when you do mow. It will stay healthier and denser, the better to keep weeds at bay.
- Don't water as often as you may have in the past. A deep weekly watering is more effective than watering daily or every other day.

- Water it at the beginning or end of the day rather than at midday.
- Leave grass clippings in place to send nutrition back into the ground and the roots. Mulching mowers are helpful but not essential.
- If you're using a gas-powered or electric lawnmower, make the task of mowing easier on yourself by eliminating acute angles from the lawn. A mower can negotiate gentle curves much better than it can turn sharp corners. Keep your mower well maintained to save fuel.
- Consider buying, or resurrecting from the back of your garage, a push mower. If the blades are kept sharp, it's an effective tool for a small lawn. And it makes that satisfying shring, shring noise a whole generation has never even heard.

THE LAWN ALTERNATIVE— A GARDEN

Instead of the endless cycle of growing and mowing a lawn, why not create a bed where you *want* plants to grow, where you don't have to trim them ever so neatly every week? Plant one garden. Plant a few.

A flower bed, or garden, may sound like more work than a lawn, but don't you believe it. This is a valid trade-off. Once a garden is established, it requires weeding and watering, sure; but you can select plants and institute practices (mulching, for example) to minimize the time it takes to keep it at its best. And if it gets away from you a bit, you can tell everyone you're going for the charming, controlled-chaos look of an English garden. It's all the rage.

.

16

think twice about vegetables

In your zeal to make your garden more than a decorative statement and, instead, feed yourself, your family, and maybe the neighborhood with some of that greenery and its fruits, you might forget you're trying to save time in the garden. Before you plant row upon row of every vegetable known to humankind, please listen first to three little words of caution: Don't Go Overboard!

Take that wonder food the tomato, for instance. There's nothing like plucking a juicy, ripe tomato and savoring it while it's still warm from the sun. That you can do with one plant. With more plants—and space and time and work—you can get a close approximation of that summertime flavor by putting by enough tomato sauce for the winter and opening jars as you need them.

Remember, though, that Paul Newman et al. do a pretty good job of

that themselves, and a couple of high-quality jars of spaghetti sauce take up a lot less space than shelf after shelf of sauce you've processed yourself. To make your own, first you have to grow the plants, lots of plants. That means preparing the soil, buying seedlings or starting them from seed; planting them; fertilizing, weeding, and watering them; keeping them safe from marauding critters and pests by erecting fences and maybe adding chemicals; and finally harvesting them.

Then you have to run them through a food mill or dunk them in hot water to remove the skins. You have to cook them, adding herbs, garlic, and spices if you want to go all the way to spaghetti sauce before you put them by.

After that comes the canning process itself, complete with unwieldy equipment, scalded fingers and nagging fears of botulism (yes, tomatoes

are a pretty safe bet; but not so with corn, apples, and other less acidic veggies and fruits). Then you have to find a dry, cool place to store all those jars.

Newman's Own is beginning to sound better and better, isn't it?

That said, there's nothing like veggies and fruits right out of your garden; well, maybe at the farmers' market, but the choice is yours. Assuming you'd like to put some homegrown food on the table, and maybe even put some of it by for the long, hard winter ahead, what kinds of vegetables and fruits (the tomato is a fruit), and how many plants of each do you want to grow? Where do you want to grow them? If you want to go the canning route, are you willing to limit your crop to one or two different veggies or fruits?

Consider the following:

- Does a large enough area of your garden receive enough sun to support the number of plants you have in mind? That means six to eight hours each sunny day. You can set aside a portion of your yard and prepare the soil so the conditions are right for growing vegetables. You can grow food in raised beds you create with two-by-fours or other materials and then fill with purchased soil (harder on the pocketbook but easier on the back).

- You can plant a single tomato plant or a climbing pea plant or two in containers and reap the benefits meal after meal. Adding a cage for them to grow in and on will help.

- How would you like fresh-grown salads? Sprinkle seeds for tender salad greens on fine soil in a container, add sunlight and water, and you can enjoy the freshest of salads day after day while the plants just keep growing. If they begin to decline, sow some more seeds to get more of these fast-maturing plants. This kind of sequential planting can reap wonderful harvests in no room at all.

- Or how about growing herbs in a strawberry jar, or purchasing a perforated plastic bag filled with strawberry plants? Using pots, boxes, or even the specially made bags, you can control the soil, amount of water and fertilizer, and pest control methods much more easily, and the yield will be manageable.

- Do you have the time to keep a vegetables garden properly tended? Maybe it's only my imagination, but I could swear that a zucchini can grow to monster proportions overnight. One day you have a four-inch-long veggie and decide to let it grow another day so it will reach its full potential; the next day you have what the English call a marrow—something that if left to its own devices could easily double as a baseball bat, and will be just about as pithy.

- Do you like the looks? Remember, unless it's somewhere out in the "back forty," a vegetable garden is part of your visible landscape. Vegetables aren't as forgiving as ornamentals when it comes to watering, and you have to be more vigilant about pests and disease if you want a good crop. Staking is essential for many plants; and mulching, drip irrigation, judicious pruning, and the like can improve your chances of a good yield.

- Will it be a project you and your children can do together? It can be great fun helping kids plant veggies, care for them, watch them grow, and then *eat* them. A pumpkin patch provides *big* returns, and jack-o'-lanterns from your own garden definitely feel more festive than those you buy at the supermarket.

- What vegetables do you *really, really* like? If you're going to grow more than a couple of plants of any given veggie, you'll have a lot to use in a short time.

All of this is not meant to discourage you. It's just a dose of reality. Now, if we could only grow chocolate . . .

17

the bubble plan—exercise 4

Now you have an idea what you *have* in your yard (the list of conditions), what you *want* in your yard (your wish list), and what you can afford to spend (your budget). Ideally, the list of what you want meshes exactly with what's already there; but sadly, that's unlikely to be the case. Let's see if you can have it all!

It's time to get out another piece of tracing paper. Tape it right over the first one on top of your base drawing. Draw new reference lines, matching them to those on the drawings underneath.

Now, using common sense and keeping in mind the constraints of sun and shade, wet and dry, time and tide, and other elements you noted on the first sheet of tracing paper, draw rough "bubbles" over areas that you think would be best suited to various purposes.

Don't be shy about "stealing" ideas from magazines or other people's gar-

dens; even grand schemes can be made to work in the spare-time garden. And don't be afraid to break away from what's already on your property. This is just an exercise to get you thinking.

While the following may seem self-evident, sometimes it's easy to overlook the obvious:

- You should be able to keep an eye on children's play areas from the house.
- As kids grow older, their needs for space in the yard will change.
- Make sure areas where you might play games are far enough from the road so that shuttlecocks (remember shuttlecocks?) won't be flying into traffic.
- Make sure sight lines are clear and that your doorway, driveway, and windows are not hidden from view by tall bushes.

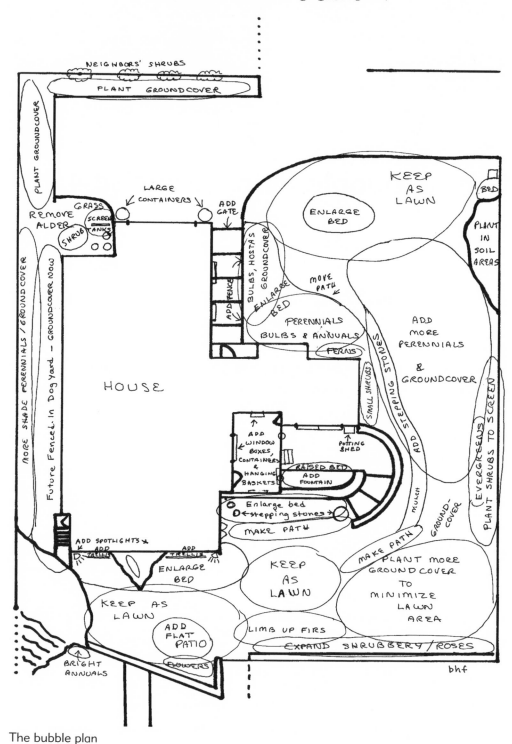

The bubble plan

- While there are shade-loving ornamental plants, fruits and vegetables almost always like lots of sun. That generally means six to eight hours a day.
- Spring bulbs can be planted under deciduous trees that won't leaf out until the bulbs have bloomed.
- Trees cast shadows in different directions at different times of day—and this changes somewhat with the seasons.
- Outdoor cooking areas should be close to a water supply and not too close to anything inflammable.
- Decks and patios should have easy access to the house and to water.
- For your comfort in hot weather, at least part of a deck or patio should be shaded, either with plants or with umbrellas or awnings.
- In northern climes, you may want these shades to be removable or retractable so you can benefit from the warmth of the sun's rays inside your home on cold winter days, or outside in spring and fall.
- Depending on what you plant, if you go on vacation during the growing season, you may have to ask someone to water your garden and harvest your vegetables.
- Dogs and cats that "go" outside are not compatible with fruits and vegetables, sandboxes, or outdoor family activities. Picking up after dogs is essential, at least on a small lot. If you have cats that spend some of their time in the garden, grow any vegetables and herbs in containers. Pack plants in so the soil is inaccessible, or cover the soil with gravel or stones. Cover sandboxes, or buy one that includes a lid.

18

the plan comes together—
exercise 5

This step is a little daunting, but it's worthwhile because it gives you a chance to refine your ideas into a workable landscape plan. If you didn't before, you now know every nook and cranny of your yard. You've thought about how you want it to look and the ways you'll use it. You're spending time to make time—and a better garden. Just plunge in and enjoy the process.

You could use a new piece of tracing paper for this next step and place it over the drawings you've already completed, creating yet another layer. Or, since all this shifting and wrinkling tracing paper is unwieldy, you could back up to the initial grid paper and tape or clip a fresh sheet of tracing paper directly over it. Keep the other sheets next to you or tacked up in front of you for reference.

Better yet, forget the tracing paper. Take one of the copies you made of your original base plan (just the buildings and other immovable objects) and draw directly on that. If you've made enough copies you can literally toss away any ideas that don't seem to be coming together the way you'd like, pull out another copy, and start fresh. Keep your notations about conditions and the bubble plan in view for reference.

Your objective now is to narrow your wish list down to a can-do list and then try to include everything on it in your drawing. Taking into account all you've learned about yourself and your property, draw a "final" plan. Create more defined outlines than in your bubble plan. Label all the areas and elements. At this point, you don't have to decide on specific plants—that comes next as you create your planting plan.

Since nothing is ever truly final, approach this exercise with an open

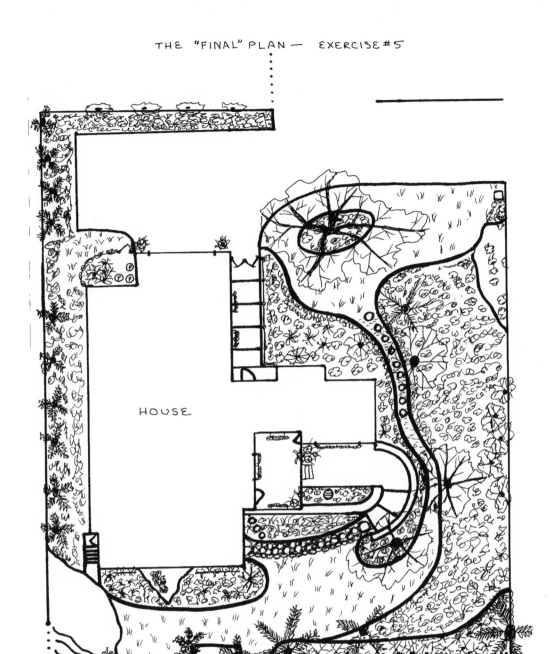

The "final" plan

mind and a willingness to be flexible. *Remember, too, that you don't have to tackle everything at once. Even a small change can have great impact.*

This drawing—your final landscape plan—is what you'll use to get started on changing or creating the look and feel of your property.

A REALITY CHECK

Looking at this most recent and final (for now) landscape plan, ask yourself the following questions:

- Can I afford the time and money to do it all at once?

- If so, do I *want* to do it all at once?

- What do I want to get done first?

- Can I fit in all the elements I had in mind?

- If not, what are the highest priority items, and what can I take off my list for now?

- Will I need help? How much, and where can I find it?

- Do I have a specific timeline—an outdoor party coming up, for example? Or simply warm weather and the prospect of gardening?

- If I do have a timeline, what can I reasonably expect to have finished when?

19

building the landscape

When you distill a landscape down to its basic building blocks, there are really only a few. Some will work better for you than others, and it's how you use them and combine them that makes your garden a success.

With the help of the landscape plan you'll soon complete, you can decide for yourself the shape and size of your lawn, garden beds, and paved areas; whether you want to include ground covers and woodland sites; which outdoor structures will serve you best; and how you want to incorporate container plantings. Then you can make it all happen. Prior to creating the plan, you should consider some of your landscape's building blocks and know what lies ahead.

HARDSCAPE IS EASY

What is hardscape anyway? It's often referred to as the "bones" of the gar-

den. It means, basically, everything that isn't a plant. It can be as immovable as a massive ledge, or as portable as a plastic planter.

Hardscape is a wonderful thing. It adds character to a garden. It provides a framework on which, and in which, your plants can look their best. No matter how beautiful the plants, without this backdrop, something is missing.

While assessing your property as part of the design exercises, you've become reacquainted with your landscape. By now, you should be looking at it in a new way and beginning to see the possibilities. When it comes to hardscape, let the following questions get you thinking:

- Is there a patio, porch, or deck? Chances are, if there is, this is where you do most of your outdoor living.

- How would it look with a cluster of potted flowers, herbs, and/or vegetables in one corner? How about a couple of window boxes to set off the architecture and add a spot of color? Does it need an awning or an umbrella to provide some shade? Maybe a trellis, or a gate to hold a flowering vine.
- Is there a large ledge or a cluster of boulders, whether left by the ice age or the contractor who built your house? How can you turn it to your advantage? Would you like to plant a pocket garden at its base? Maybe adding a bench nearby would make it more welcoming, or you could add other rocks and make the boulders the focus of a rock garden.

You get the idea. Ask questions and then find the answers that suit you and the way you live. Before long, you'll have a better idea of what you want to do with the bones of your landscape.

"PLANTING" ROCKS

You've seen—or godforbid, have in your garden—rocks that look as if they've been plunked down for no good reason. They sit uncomfortably on top of the ground looking like misfits at a junior high dance. You almost expect them to start fidgeting and fall off their perches.

Rocks look great in the landscape, but they must be integrated into both the plan *and* the ground. Pretend they're icebergs and bury about two-thirds of each rock below the soil. Unfortunately, mounding soil around the rock—unless you do it in a large area, and that's way too much work—doesn't do the trick. Take a little time, and your efforts will be rewarded with rocks that look as though they've struggled up through the earth to see the light of day in *your* garden.

LANDSCAPE BY DESIGN

How do you design a garden from scratch? Follow your own inclinations and remember the basics.

Gardens next to buildings or patios; around trees, mailboxes, trellises, or other objects; or connecting various elements of the property are more appealing than a circle or island carved out willy-nilly in the middle of a lawn. Ideally, structures, gardens, furnishings, etc. should have a feeling of cohesiveness that ties them all together.

Generally speaking, curves in the garden are more pleasing and feel more natural than straight lines. You can integrate straight edges into some garden areas, along a fence or sidewalk for example, and then end with a curve; or you can create a formal and angular design using all straight lines and right angles. The choice is yours. The overall effect you achieve should take into account the style of your home, how you'll be using your property, and where the garden will be.

Pathways are more enticing if they wind and curve towards a house. If they "disappear" behind a bush or structure and then reemerge, better still. This effective design device is known as "conceal and reveal."

Water elements can be messy and time consuming and draw pests. They can also be wonderful accents in the garden—just know what you're getting into.

Think in terms of outdoor rooms and hallways or living/working/traveling spaces. A garden should have "walls" and a "roof," and plantings can serve both purposes.

A pergola or trellis adds a sense of volume and definition to a garden area.

Along a drip line, spreading stone or gravel instead of plants saves your garden from being beaten down by water off the roof. If possible, plantings should begin outside the drip line, at least two feet away from any structure.

Adjacent areas should have some connection to each other; seating next to the cookout area or the swing set near (but not too near) the pool, for example.

Balance and a sense of scale are important. The major elements of a garden have a virtual weight and volume—the sense you get from their size and shape. In adjoining or opposite areas, they can be placed in a strictly symmetrical arrangement, or they can be combined so that the balance is maintained without symmetry. Symmetry is more formal than the balanced-but-asymmetrical look, but it doesn't have to be boring. Both are legitimate approaches, and the style of your home can be a good guiding factor.

You might not notice if a garden, or some plants in a garden, are out of scale. It will just feel wrong. Plants that are too big or too small for their space detract from the overall effect. Smaller plants may eventually grow to a size that would improve the scale, but it's harder to prune or cut larger plants to suit smaller needs.

There's no need to rush. If, based on your landscape decisions, you feel you'd like to add or subtract garden space, why not start with one area and see how it goes? Get a feel for the amount of work involved in both creating the garden and tending it, as well as the way the new space works for you and your family. Then, using what you've learned, move on to the next spot you want to change. As long as you have a plan, you can take on the project one step at a time.

KEEP OFF THE GRASS

If you want to create a new garden, or change the dimensions and shape of one that's already in place, it will probably mean either taking away or adding grass. Because both jobs are somewhat time consuming, think carefully about where you want the boundaries of your gardens to be.

Removing grass is a drag, but if you're adding a garden where a lawn has been, all the grass within that edging has to be removed, roots and all, if possible. Otherwise, you'll end up with stubborn clumps of lawn amidst the plantings—and that, believe me, is even more of a drag. Before you begin, make sure the grass is cut short; that way there's less to remove.

How do you get rid of sod? There's the hard way and the not-so-hard way. To do it the hard way, cut a sheet of plastic that will cover the grass and matches your new garden's contour. Weigh it down with soil or rocks, and wait. Then, after the grass dies, remove the soil and rocks and dig up the nasty brown grass. Note that this still requires digging.

The not-so-hard way is more straightforward. Put a tarp, wheelbarrow, or open trash bag beside where you want to remove the grass and, using a flat spade or a half-moon edger, cut along the new garden contour. The next step, since you need to get rid of *all* the grass within the soon-to-be garden, is to cut a line two or three inches away from the edge, within the garden contour.

A spade width at a time, remove the sod between these two lines and put it on the tarp or in the wheelbarrow or trash container. Then, cut a new line several inches within your new border, and repeat this process until all the grass is gone. This is obviously time consuming, but is easier than the kill and lift method, which adds another step.

As soon as possible after you're done, take away the sod you've removed, or the tarp, etc. will turn the lawn yellow. Since grass is heavy, you may have to do this in installments.

You might be tempted to go the gas-powered tiller route, and it could be that turning over the area mechanically is the only viable alternative if you're turning a massive portion of your lawn into garden or another use. Just be aware that overtilling the soil can change its structure for the worse; and if you turn under the grass, some of it might find its way back up to the surface and invade your new bed.

What should you do with the sod you've removed? I'd like to say that if you take it out carefully, you can use it to patch up other areas in your garden. Unfortunately, you'd have to make sure the fit is right and dig out the area so the edges match in height. Since using the not-so-hard method results in smallish pieces of sod, you can put it in a compost bin and wait till it's well cooked before using it on the garden; or you can take it to a dump where there's a composting area. If you happen to have a few acres of woods, you can spread it out in a shady area with the knowledge that it will become part of the forest floor, or you can give it to a neighbor who's looking for clean fill.

To add grass (if you must), rake what will be the new lawn area smooth. Select a high-quality seed in the same color and type to match the rest of your lawn; and follow the planting directions, including the timing for your part of the country. Protect it from intrusion by people and pets while the grass is getting started. Then water and fertilize as recommended until your new lawn is established and afterwards as needed to keep it healthy and green. And finally, mow, mow, mow . . .

MAKING YOUR BED

After completing the landscape design exercises, you'll have a general idea of where you want each garden bed to be. Now's the time to decide what shape you want one garden (or all of them if you're going whole hog). If you're using space where you already grow plants, all you have to decide is whether or not you like that particular garden's shape and size. If you're turning lawn or some other surface into a garden area, you'll have to decide the dimensions and contours.

Here's how to get started when you want to change or create a garden bed: On the ground, lay out the shape you want. This is a crucial step that really affects how your new garden will look. Some people advise using a hose to do this, and if you can get it to lie flat and stay still, that's a fine option. Since they're more flexible and lighter, I prefer using hefty, brightly colored pieces of rope or clothesline—hefty and bright so you can see it and get an idea of what the new outline of your garden will be; rope or clothesline because both are more malleable than a rubber hose.

A little contemplation before you dig can save you time. Once the contours are determined and the garden is planted, it's easier to expand the cultivated area than to turn it back into turf. Either way, it's better to do it right the first time than to chip away at it bit by bit, year after year. Unless you're really sure exactly where you want to plant a garden, put down the rope guideline where you think the planting's edges should be, and then sit back and wait a few days. Look at the area inside and outside the rope from various angles and at different times of day. Imagine a garden on one side and a lawn or other surface (pavers, ground cover, etc.) on the other. Ask yourself the following questions:

Will this garden be visible enough from your indoor and/or outdoor living areas to make it worthwhile; or, if it's a utilitarian cutting garden or vegetable patch, is it a little more visible than you might like? Is it out of the family's and pets' traffic flow? How much sun does it get? This will affect your plant choices. How's the drainage? Does the shape please you, and is it simple and classic enough that it won't feel stale in a year or two? Will it be easy to tend? Is it accessible for weeding, cutting flowers, or picking vegetables?

Once you've decided on the contours of your bed, it's almost time to dig in. But wait: Check the weather and the ground. Digging in the dirt before the soil has warmed up a bit in the spring can damage its texture. Pick up a handful of soil from your yard and work it through your fingers. Is it quite damp? Does it clump together? Then it's the wrong time to start digging. Once the changing weather has produced a string of consistently warm days, try this test again—and again if necessary. Eventually you'll pick up a handful of earth and, with just a little prodding, it will crumble and fall through your fingers. It's become friable, which means that now you can begin.

If the occasion calls for removing bits of lawn, roll up your shirtsleeves, put on a sturdy pair of shoes, get out your shovel, and go to work. Maybe you can convince someone to help you at this stage, since it's a time-consuming operation.

If you've dug up grass to get to this point, what you have is a brown, neatly edged, shallow hole in your yard. It's time to fill that hole with a garden. But how?

You should first raise the soil level to replace what you've removed. Using a spade or a garden fork, fluff up what's there. If you didn't have much grass to remove, or if its roots were quite shallow, the soil that remains might miraculously fill the depression in the ground. Nonetheless, adding a layer of compost at this point will give your new garden a boost. If you have some compost of your own, and it's ready to go, fine. Since we're pressed for time, though, it's probably easier to purchase compost at the nearest garden center.

If the hole left when you've dug out your garden area is deeper than you can fill with a little fluffing, you might need quite a bit to raise the level. You can purchase and add topsoil, a more economical choice than compost. Compost will enrich your garden and improve the texture, whereas topsoil probably doesn't offer as many nutrients. If you use packaged topsoil, why not add some compost into the mix as well?

You can often buy topsoil and compost in quantity at a discount. Any bags that are left over can be used in other areas of your garden. However, only do this if you have a place to store them or you know you'll use them. I know all too well that leftover bags look unsightly piled up at the edge of a yard all summer and into the fall.

Spread the soil and/or compost evenly over the ground and work it in, breaking up any large clumps and removing any stones you encounter.

On your forays to select plants for your garden, remember that spacing them closer than recommended takes more time and costs more, but it creates a better display in less time. Using larger plants is also a way to make a garden look more established and may even cost less in the long run. One big plant might be less expensive than the three small ones that would ordinarily go in its space. No matter what their size, though, several plants of one kind are more pleasing and have a greater impact on the design than just one lone specimen.

CUTTING AN EDGE

On your visits to public gardens, or private gardens that get it right, notice the areas where lawn meets garden, where driveway meets plantings, where patio or porch meets shrubbery. The lines are clean, aren't they? There's a little edging or notch where one area meets another. Plants can spill over these edges, but the spillage is controlled; and somehow you just know the edges are underneath there all the time. It lends order to the landscape; and, best of all, it keeps one area from encroaching on another.

The choices for delimiting gardens are as limitless as the gardening and hardware industry can manage. There are pavers and stone, plastic edging, rubber hoses that create edges and water your plants at the same time, cute little wrought iron fences, mini-pickets, railroad ties, and just plain soil. Which one is the best kind of edge for you? That would be the *easiest* kind. Here's a look at some of the options.

Stones and pavers are an open invitation for weeds and grass to become lodged in their interstices (great word, interstices). If you don't mind scuffed knuckles or bent kitchen knives, then by all means go for the calming look of natural stone, cobblestones, or brick (or faux versions of same) to separate your lawn and garden. Just be aware that there's a cost involved—your time; and of course, stone isn't cheap.

Our house has a small, raised patio of slate bordered by an old, lichen-covered stone wall. Between the top of the wall and the slate paving is a nice little bed of good, deep soil in which I grow all manner of things. Separating this elevated bed and the patio is a row of cobblestones. I have a real love/hate relationship with both the stones and the slabs of slate, even though there isn't much of either of them. They're cool and attractive in the summer, but I'm constantly battling the volunteers and weeds that grow up in the cracks. Sometimes it's grass, with which I'm heartless; but when it's a columbine or a violet, I can't bear to pull it out but pretend it's an accent I meant to have in that very spot.

There's precedent for this. No less a personage than the Queen of England has interstices (there's that word again) in the slate pavers behind Balmoral Castle in Scotland, and these chinks in the patio are planted with herbs and little flowers. If you choose stone as an edging, don't choose much of it—and think cottagey and quaint, as no doubt the queen often does.

Those little plastic or wrought iron fences really don't do anything to sepa-rate one area from another, except visually. You still have to create an edge—a little trench works fine—and then trim around the fencing, which can be time consuming.

Railroad ties aren't as popular as they once were. Some are permeated with tar or nasty preservatives, and even those tend to splinter and fall apart after a few years. If they're elevated, you can't mow right up to them, so they require the attentions of a trimmer. However, if they're set far enough into the ground, you can save trimming time by mowing over them.

Plastic edgers that you pound into the ground can look good and, if set low enough, will allow the edge of the mower to reach up to them. In the north, they tend to dislodge after a couple of frosty winters. The tubes with holes for attaching to a hose are appeal-ing, but watering the garden that way is a haphazard, all-or-nothing affair.

Probably the best edging is a cleanly dug border. Using a square spade or a half-moon edger, follow the contours of your garden bed and create a little V-shaped notch that separates one area from another. It looks neat and keeps mulch confined to the garden.

PAVED AREAS

Your climate and the way you use your yard will directly affect how much of it you want paved. Paving can be a solid bed of asphalt on a driveway. It can also be a patio, walkway, steps, or edging of slate or fieldstone, synthetic materials, gravel, manufactured stone, concrete, bricks, or granite. Using paving doesn't have to make a property look like a parking lot; in fact, used judiciously, it can be an attractive and effective addition to the landscape.

Paving underfoot, especially under a canopy of trees, can often cool down the feel of a property. Think of damp, mossy bricks in a shady Savannah courtyard.

In the sun, it can heat things up. Think of bricks baking in the heat, reflecting the warmth right into the surrounding area.

Paving offers a sturdy and less buggy base for outdoor furniture. Of course, if made of the right materials, it also provides a durable place to park cars.

Expense is often a consideration when purchasing pavers. Granite, for example, can break the bank pretty quickly. Plastics and other synthetics are relatively inexpensive, but the look just isn't the same. Using less of the real thing might be a better investment.

CONTAINERS

The pots and planters you use have a great impact on your landscape. They don't have to be expensive to look great. Even the faux terra-cotta and stone planters look fine, although they might not last as long as the real thing. On the other hand, they just might fare better in the heating-thawing cycles of winter.

If you like a little variety, or if your needs change due to entertaining, games in the yard, or some other reason, the great thing about containers is you can move them. That's a legitimate argument for using the lightweight pots made of synthetic materials.

Large containers look more impressive and, better still, need less frequent watering and fertilizing than smaller pots—although they still need more than a garden bed does. If your containers are different sizes, position them with the smaller pots in front. You can also stage your containers by placing those that will be in the back of the display on bricks or special little "legs" sold for that purpose.

Many decorative pottery planters are glazed in a wonderful choice of hues. These are very appealing and generally sturdy, except that they need to be taken inside during the winter in colder climates. They give a property a stately, more formal look. Natural materials, terra-cotta for example, lend a more casual atmosphere to the landscape.

Urns are another choice. They come in all colors, sizes, materials, and levels of ornament. Using a really big urn or two makes a fantastic design statement, but the price may be daunting.

With containers, as in the rest of the landscape, scale is an important consideration. A four-foot-high planter might look out of place beside a tiny Cape Cod–style house, while at a large home, a smattering of little pots on the front steps might look like a halfhearted effort. When the scale, material, and plants are all in balance, the containers look neither too big nor too small; they're just right.

20

help! the sequel:
do you need professional help?

After you've come up with a working landscape plan, you need to ask yourself if you want, or are able, to do everything yourself to get started, and then to keep it looking good. Think about the complexity of your property and projects, how able and skilled you are at the various jobs that will go into making and keeping your landscape the way you want it, how much time you're willing to put in, and the money you're prepared to spend.

Is it realistic to expect to do your own tree work? Do you know how to keep safe while you're up in the treetops or sawing a heavy branch with an even heavier chainsaw?

Do you know how to build walls or fences? Can you dig deep holes? Are you construction savvy enough to build a deck or a trellis?

If you don't yet know how to do these things, do you want to learn? If

so, are there lessons or classes available nearby that fit into your budget and schedule?

MAKING THE CHOICES

Depending on your answers to the above questions, you might decide to design, build, and tend every portion of your property yourself, perhaps with the help of friends and family. On the other hand, someday—or even today—you may decide to take advantage of the services of a professional. It will save you time and cost you money, but you may eventually save in other areas as a result. The choice is yours.

Maybe you want to hire a landscaper, landscape designer, or landscape architect for the initial planning and planting and/or for subsequent maintenance.

What's the difference between landscapers, landscape designers, and landscape architects? Generally speaking, it's a matter of training and, to some degree, experience and skill. It designates the complexity of the design services they offer. It also refers to the amount of hands-on work you can expect versus how much will be contracted out to others.

Landscapers can come in and mow your lawn, plant your garden, limb up or take down a tree, set stones and paving, and do general yard work. They can also offer advice and sell you plants. It's likely they have more on-the-job experience than formal training.

Landscape designers look at your property, ask questions, and come up with a design and plant selections. You can either take it from there or hire the designer to complete and/or subcontract the work. They have studied and practiced landscape design, and many are associated with garden centers.

Landscape architects have a degree in landscape architecture and are certified and licensed. They seldom do the hands-on work themselves, except in special circumstances; but because of their training, their designs often feature a higher level of sophistication and attention to detail than you'd find from other sources. They can line up the workers who can then implement their designs.

Arborists, carpenters, and masons are other skilled workers you may want to hire for portions of your landscape work. It's important to know your limits and recognize that there are those who can do in practically no time what it would take you weeks to accomplish; and the work they produce might be better and last longer. Once you get a feel for what has to be done, you'll find it easier to know when to call in the experts so you can spend your time elsewhere.

RIGHT UP FRONT

If you're flummoxed or want to save time by hiring a professional for all or part of the work, be sure you find an individual or firm that suits your personality and your pocketbook. Many will come to see you and assess your property at no charge for the initial visit. They should provide references; and before you do any hiring or sign any contracts, you'd be wise to take a look at other properties they've landscaped or designed and talk to the homeowners about their experiences.

Even if you decide to call in a professional, it makes sense to spend the time first to get to know your landscape and your expectations for it. It will help the process go more smoothly and save you time and probably money. You'll be more likely to make the right choices for your garden on the first try, instead of having to make expensive and time-consuming changes later on.

part three

Time to Get Growing

21

planning the plants

Which plants will work for you? This question involves more than asking what will grow in your garden. This is when some of those answers you came up with earlier become relevant and useful. What do you like? What do you want to grow? What don't you want to grow? And so on.

You've narrowed down the choices by thinking what colors, sizes, and shapes you might want in various parts of the garden and how much you want to spend. You've even made note of some species of plant you like. When you create your planting plan, you'll determine the numbers you'll need.

MAKE IT EASY
ON YOURSELF—
AND THE PLANTS

Here's something else to consider: To make gardening more productive and improve your plants' chances of survival, select those that fit the conditions you can provide. No matter where you garden, there are plenty of fabulous species that will look great in your garden without pampering, so why not choose them instead of their temperamental cousins?

Your selections can be as varied as you care to make them, within the limits of time, money, location, and space. Just read the labels carefully when planning and planting. Knowing which plants you're able to grow narrows the field, although there will *always* be more plants you'll want to try but don't have room or time for, even within that narrower field. That's one of the temptations gardeners face each year.

While you can amend soil to balance out its acidity and alkalinity, or grow some sun-loving plants in partial shade, or water endlessly in dry areas, sometimes it's best to go with the flow, or *grow* with the flow. If you have acid soil, then why not grow plants that love acid soil? With all the wonderful shade-loving plants, why not select those instead of sun worshippers? If you live where rain is scarce, why not try xeriscaping (landscaping with plants that can store up their own water or do without to a large degree)?

If you fight plants' natural inclinations, whether by putting them in the wrong soil or light or simply by choosing the wrong species, you'll all be miserable. While you might be able to nurse some along as they'll struggle through year after year, in the long run it really doesn't pay to buy plants you have to coddle. And if one doesn't thrive, swallow your pride and your qualms and toss it or give it away.

The flip side is, if you put the right plant in the right place, a near magical transformation occurs. It grows. It thrives. And it's beautiful!

We all have favorites, and our favorites can change depending on whether or not they're successful in our gardens. When we moved to Maine, the back of my car was filled with three cat carriers (complete with extremely vocal cats) and a large rosebush that had done beautifully since I'd bought it through a fancy catalogue several years before. I planted it immediately, and it died of natural causes during its first Maine winter! Now I happily grow roses from the nursery around the corner.

The moral of this tale: If you can't seem to grow a particular kind of plant, you'll soon learn to love the plants you can grow.

WHAT'S HOT? WHAT'S NOT?

There are almost as many fashions in the plant world as in the world of fashion. Just listen to the buzz around the garden center and you'll hear a real hubbub of interest around the current introductions. They excite seasoned gardeners who want to try something different. Frequently, these recently developed plants are more expensive than old standards, but they're often superior in one way or another—color, vigor, length of bloom time, spread, disease resistance, hardiness, more tolerance for shade or hot sun, ease of maintenance, etc.

These improvements can mean an easier time in the garden for all of us, so it pays to take a look at new varieties, including the award winners touted as superstars of the plant world. These are fun to try, but if you're pinching pennies, why not grow last year's top picks? The plants are just as good as they were a year ago, but the prices often become more reasonable once the spotlight shifts to the newest celebrities. Before you decide to plant one of these newcomers in your garden, however, consider whether it's really what you want

Kousa Dogwood

ful your flowering plants are, periodic deadheading (removing faded flowers) can extend the blooming period for many perennials (and annuals, too, for that matter). It takes a little time, but you'll enjoy the rewards. Every two or three years, you should divide many of your perennials to keep them healthy (see chapter 29, "Keeping the Plants in Check"). It's a great way to increase your collection at no cost and in very little time.

and if it fits the conditions you can offer it.

PRACTICALLY PERFECT PLANTS

Countless plants are available to home gardeners. For landscape planning purposes, they generally include annuals and perennials, bulbs, ground covers, shrubs, trees, and wildflowers. For the purposes of this book, I'll include plants that are currently in my garden—plus a few from my wish list.

Since some catalogues and growers use latinized names exclusively, I'm listing the plants by their common names and adding some simplified botanical (Latin) names. In some cases, the familiar and botanical names are the same; and in others, the Latin names are commonly used.

Once you've planted your garden, remember that no matter how wonder-

WHEN IS A PLANT A PERENNIAL?

Since it means a plant hardy enough to take what your particular winter can dish out, the word *perennial* refers to different plants in different places. In reality, what's considered a perennial (that is to say, hardy) in South Carolina is a lot different from what's a perennial in Minnesota. That's why the Department of Agriculture's hardiness zone map is an indispensable tool. Of course, you might be able to fudge a little, maybe increasing your choices by an entire zone in a warm, sunny spot in your garden. Beware the occasional harsh winter, though; you may lose some of your "perennials," even in your mini "tropical" ecosystem. It's the chance you take.

It gets a little more complicated. Take two plants of a species that's hardy in all U.S. zones. Plant one in Georgia and one in New Hampshire, both on the same day. Guess which one's going to come up earlier. It's a cinch the one you plant in the South will come up sooner. If it's a continuous bloomer, it might last longer in the season there, too, since the first frost will most probably occur later. If you plant in rainy Washington State you'll have different results than if your garden is in arid New Mexico—and not just because of temperature differences. Even if you water regularly, humidity or the lack thereof affects what you can grow and whether what you grow will flourish.

In other words, keep more than your zone in mind when selecting perennials for *your* garden. Consider climate, altitude, humidity, winds, soil conditions, and other variables.

A GARDENFUL OF PERENNIALS

The world of perennials includes plants with roots, rhizomes, and bulbs. Technically, trees, shrubs, and even lawn grasses are perennials, too; but for our purposes we'll use the word to describe herbaceous perennials. These are plants that grow on green rather than woody stems and usually die back to the ground in winter; but because their roots stay alive despite the cold, they survive to bloom another year, and another.

Perennials can spread among other plants as ground covers or climb high above the rest of the garden as vines. It's an old adage that perennials crawl the first year, walk the second year, and run the third year. If conditions are right, it's usually smooth sailing from there on as they fill our gardens with beautiful and dependable foliage and flowers.

Here are some of my favorite herbaceous perennials to whet your appetite. Not so coincidentally, all of them are growing in my small yard. Fortunately they're hardy "Downeast," which means they're also hardy in lots of other places. Some have great colors, others like to bloom and bloom, and most tend to be trouble free (I wouldn't have it any other way). Then there are those that are simply perfect in every way.

- **Monkshood** (*Aconitum*) was in our yard when we bought the house. I found out later that it's extremely poisonous, but fortunately the pets don't seem interested anyway. It grows tall and straight with fringelike foliage that appears early in spring. The brilliant blue flowers, aptly named for their hooded shape, shine brightly in my so-called woodland garden. Aconitum is also available in shades of yellow, white, and pink.
- **Lady's mantle** (*Alchemilla mollis*) was thought to have religious or magical significance because of the way water beads up on its

leaves. This plant tolerates some shade. To deadhead it, hold the stem that bears the flower (the scape) near where it meets the leaves and pull while twisting.

- **Columbine** (*Aquilegia*) is a wildflower that's been cultivated into many interesting colors and more exotic shapes than the "original." Since there tend to be several showy blooms open at the same time, these funnel-shaped flowers with long, thin "spurs" rise above their soft-green, lobed foliage to create a bouquet right there in your garden.

- **Artemisia** provides a silvery, low mound of lacy foliage that adds interest to the front of the border. It seems that no matter what the conditions, it just keeps on going.

- **Astilbe** is easy to grow and is graceful in the garden. Whether dwarf or tall, these exceptional plants flower from June through September and grow in the shade or in sun if kept moist enough. The stems have touches of red and burgundy, and their delicate plumes of flowers look great in massed plantings. They even look good as they dry right on the plant—no need to deadhead.

- **Heather** (*Calluna*) is a lovely and showy, nicely textured plant in pink or white that harkens back to my Scottish roots. I always keep a few around the ledge garden, although there's a bit of culture clash going on with the Siberian iris and Korean dogwood nearby.

- **Coreopsis** comes in a great many varieties, and growers seem to introduce new ones daily. 'Moonbeam', a pale yellow Coreopsis, is especially popular. There are even pinks and reds, as well as doubles, available.

- **Bleeding heart** (*Dicentra*) is an old favorite that reliably produces pink, red, or white pendulous flowers in shady or partly shady spots. In its traditional form, *D. spectabilis*, it blooms spectacularly (hence the genus name) in the spring and then dies back. Newer bleeding hearts, such as *Dicentra* 'Luxuriant', bloom from May into October above dainty divided leaves.

- **Hardy geranium**, or cranesbill, flowers profusely in shades of blue, pink, and purple on delicate foliage. It's easy to grow in sunny or partially shady areas of the garden and divides well. This true geranium should not be confused with the immensely popular Pelargonium. That sturdy flowering plant commonly known as geranium is generally an annual, although in my house a number of different varieties happily spend winters inside waiting to bloom again in containers each summer.

- **Christmas rose or Lenten rose** (*Helleborus*) blooms very early or very late, depending on how you look at it and where you are. The leaves on these garden treasures are evergreen in most areas.
- **Daylily** (*Hemerocallis*), sometimes spelled as two words (day lily) is among the most enjoyable and easiest perennials to grow. The varieties of daylily—now approaching 50,000 in number—come in an enormous range of colors from creamy whites through yellows and oranges to darkest reds. These long-lasting plants with their short-lived flowers spread each year and are easily divided so you can start new clumps throughout your garden. Include some varieties that continue to send forth flowers all season ('Stella d'Oro' is one that's readily available), as well as some that bloom early, in mid-season, and late. To add an attractive new dimension to an entryway, plant one of the more fragrant varieties of daylily beside the door. Create a wonderful interplay of colors and textures in the back of the border by combining tall daylilies in many

shades and various bloom times with some brilliant blue perennials (monkshood or delphinium) and spiky white veronica; and maybe add some silvery plants, such as the low-growing lamb's ears or mounded artemisia, to the front of the garden to heighten the effect. Each year, the display will increase in breadth and intensity, and you'll enjoy the show.

- **Coral bells** or **Alumroot** (*Heuchera*) likes part sun or shade. This compact plant features tiny flowers held aloft on thin stems above attractive, gently lobed foliage.
- **Hosta** is another dependable and incredibly varied perennial that is easily propagated through root division. One plant can soon become many, and the individuals will spread every year. Hostas do well in shade or partial shade, and those with white markings on their leaves shine nicely in the evening. There are delightfully fragrant varieties and interesting foliage colors in all sizes of hostas. The flowers are in shades of white and lavender.
- **Iris** comes in all heights and an astonishing range of colors and combinations. The sword-leaved plants spread, and the rhizomes can be readily divided and re-

planted. Flag, Siberian, Japanese, or tall bearded iris are several of the best-known species. They all look great growing in front of a wall or in ever-expanding clumps in the herbaceous border.

- **Lavender** (*Lavandula angustifolia*) can offer a sense of being transported to the Cotswolds or Provence. 'Munstead' and 'Hidcote' are hardier than some other lavenders. The scent and color are amazing!

- **Sea lavender** (*Limonium latifolium*), with its low, coppery leaves and tiny, dusty-lavender flowers along thin, branching stems, grows precariously yet successfully by the sea. However, like the lady's slipper orchid and others, it doesn't transplant easily from the wild. Purchase your plants, and you'll have stems that dry with no fuss at all to provide a long-lasting decorative accent for your home.

- **Phlox** (*Phlox paniculata*) is tall, cheerful, and bright; and newer varieties are resistant to the powdery mildew that blights some members of this species. Phlox also comes in dwarf varieties and the creeping *P. subulata*, familiarly known as moss pinks.

- **Solomon's seal** (*Polygonatum*) bears graceful, creamy white flowers that hang from long,

arching stems. It grows well in full shade (be careful it doesn't take over the woodland garden) and bears up to wind and weather—and even salt spray.

- **Primrose** (*Primula*) is a cheerful precursor to spring. The colors come straight out of a box of crayons. Although these are generally hardy perennials, those you buy in the supermarket might not make it through to the following year. Nonetheless, we sometimes just need that touch of spring before anything else blooms.

- **Black-eyed Susan** (*Rudbeckia*), sometimes called coneflower, is tall and vibrant and looks good in the middle or back of the border, depending on the height of the other plants you choose. Ask your nursery staff, since some varieties can be invasive; others are great.

- **Stonecrop** (*Sedum*) creates a dense, spreading carpet of succulent leaves in spring and then blooms later in the season; but you can leave the flowers on to provide winter interest in the garden. There are lots of varieties, one of which my father called "cat's tongue" because of its rough oval leaves.

- **Blue-eyed grass** (*Sisyrinchium*) looks like a little clump of grass but offers a surprise—perky, bright-blue flowers that go on for months. It needs little maintenance, but be careful not to dig it out of your flower bed thinking it's a clump of grass that's migrated beyond the lawn.

- **Lamb's ears** (*Stachys*) is adorable, if only for its common name; but it has more going for it: The fuzzy, gray-green leaves on this low-growing plant create a wonderful counterpoint in the front of a flower bed. The clumps spread a little further each year, multiplying your investment. Try it and you'll be smitten.

- **Globeflower** (*Trollius*) has blooms that, in the yellow varieties, look for all the world like giant double buttercups. This plant ranges from medium-low mounds to tall, and some have ivory or orange flowers. It likes a range of light conditions from full sun to partial shade and looks great in mixed arrangements of cut flowers.

- **Speedwell** (*Veronica*) offers long-lasting and attractive white, pink, or blue flower spikes that have an exotic look to them in both the border and in bouquets. Like astilbe, varieties available range from dwarf to tall; unlike astilbe, it prefers full sun.

FERNS

Some perennials may produce only miniscule flowers or no flowers at all, but we love them for their foliage and their dependability. Ferns, for example, can add a lush, rain-forest-like feel to even the most northern gardens. They come in many sizes, from tiny to huge, and are available in all shades of green. In the right conditions—rich, moist soil in shade (or sometimes even sun)—ferns multiply and spread. I only have two species:

- **Japanese painted fern** (*Athyrium niponicum*) is showy, with dark-red and silver accents. It comes up a little later than some of the others, so don't give up hope and plant something else in its place.

- **Ostrich fern** (*Matteuccia struthiopteris*) is your classic fern. It's also edible: The first curled fronds or "fiddleheads" are a delicacy—if you can grow enough and can bring yourself to cut them. Instead, why not let them grow and spread in a glen or on a shady bank?

SHRUBS

There's a shrub, or woody perennial, for just about anywhere in your garden. Some have flowers and berries; some are evergreens. Some have graceful branching habits, while others lend themselves to trimming and shaping. Low-growing shrubs such as some junipers can be used as ground covers. Lilac, viburnum, mock orange, quince, roses, and other shrubs can have beautifully scented flowers. When they're brought inside as cut flowers, however, the aroma can become overwhelming for some people. Some varieties of the most highly scented plants have no scent at all—go figure.

Here are the woody perennials, small and not so small, growing in my garden:

- **Daphne** is a delightfully fragrant, well-mannered plant. My 'Carol Mackie' has creamy-edged leaves, and early each summer it's covered with thick clusters of tiny, waxy flowers that vary from lavender to pink to white. I actually have two small daphnes. The first was on sale, probably because it's a twisted, stunted version of a grand plant. I bought the second one to keep the poor thing company. They're both quite small but bloom beautifully year after year.

- **Hydrangea** can have lacy caps or giant "snowballs" for flowers. It can climb high on two-story trellises or grow into a hefty shrub. The colors range from whites through blues and violets to bright pinks, and the hues can be manipulated through soil additives and other means—but, truly, why bother? That's for people who have a whole lot more time on their hands than we do. The flowers dry beautifully with no effort whatsoever.

- **Holly** (*Ilex*) offers branches full of flowers and then berries, as long as you have a female plant or plants—and a male nearby. If you want to teach your children about the birds and the bees, this is a very subtle way to start.

- **Kerria japonica,** with its cheerful yellow flowers (I like the doubles) and graceful, arching branches, has long been one of my favorite shrubs.

- **Lilacs** come in so many sizes and shades of white, pink, blue, purple, and even yellow that it's hard to choose. If you have plenty of room, just pick the one that appeals to you. Dwarf varieties grow more slowly and are fine if space is a consideration. I have a 'Miss Kim' that threatens to grow way too big, so my husband, "The Mad Pruner," trims it back just after it blooms in the spring.

- **Bayberry** (*Myrica*) is tough and has fruit whose scent is valued by candle makers as well as gardeners. In our yard, several bayberries grow above an old stone wall just a couple of feet from the ocean at high tide. Tough indeed!

- **Potentilla** can become a nicely rounded bush several feet in height. It's considered versatile because it does as well in hot, dry locations such as along the foggy Maine shore. Its small leaves add interest, but the charming flowers—primarily yellow, but also available in white or pink—are the stars of the show. This can become a nicely rounded bush several feet in height.

- The name **"Rhododendron"** can cover a lot of territory. Azaleas, plants with small, often deciduous leaves, are technically rhododendrons, as are the broadleaved, big-blossomed plants we ordinarily think of as rhododendrons (and they're all in the heath family). The large-leaved plants sometimes suffer in winter from desiccation or dehydration of the leaves, so make sure the plants are thoroughly watered in the fall before the ground freezes. Treating the leaves with a special spray helps them survive.

- **Rosa** (a rose by any other name) can be wild and wooly or terribly civilized. Selecting carefree roses will save you no end of time and aggravation. Before you make the investment, check out a rose's hardiness, pest and disease resistance, light and soil preferences, growth habit, degree of thorniness, and, of course, its color. Some people who grow these legendary plants envelop themselves in a mystique that intimidates those who are simply thinking of planting a rose or two or three. Do a little homework and think about what you want out of a rose; you'll be fine.

SHRUB WISH LIST

While I don't have them in my Maine garden, *yet,* I'm hankering after several world-class shrubs that have grown well for me in the past.

- **Viburnum** is a plant with perfectly gorgeous flowers that keep on blooming for months, as well as fall color, colorful fruit, and, in some cases, an amazing aroma.

- **Meyer lemon** and other small citrus trees make wonderful, scented additions to the patio, and in winter they are well-behaved decorative accents inside, as well as a source for fresh fruit.

- **Mountain laurel** (*Kalmia*) is the state flower of Pennsylvania, but that's only part of the reason I like it so much. Its clusters of cup-shaped white flowers with tinges of pink brighten the spring and early summer garden; and the waxy leaves are evergreen.

- **Witch hazel** blooms in early spring or late fall, depending on the variety; and its curly yellow flowers add amazing spots of color when most other deciduous plants are bare.

GRASSES

We aren't talking about lawns here but, rather, ornamental grasses. Ornamental grasses can be, well, very ornamental. They can be tall and wave in the summer breezes and then look decorative all winter if left undisturbed, or they can be short and highly variegated so they practically glow in the dark. Try to avoid the more invasive varieties, though.

While we're on the subject: To grow grass for your lawn, select seed that is suited to your region. To fill in bare spots, try to match the grass you already have so the color and growth rate will be the same.

GLORIOUS GROUND COVERS

These perennials flower. They flow. They flourish. They're absolutely fabulous. They look polished without ever needing a trim and, once established, keep weeds from ever showing their faces. For every square foot of ground cover you plant, there's a foot less lawn to mow. They also need less water and fewer chemicals. What's not to love?

Well, maybe one thing: You generally shouldn't walk on ground covers. If you want a green surface you can move around on, it should probably be lawn. If the area you're planting simply serves as a pathway from here to there, consider "planting" stepping stones among the ground cover for a wonderful look that at the same time affords access to other parts of your garden.

Ground covers are the perfect solutions for a lot of problem areas: steep banks, for example. Some are wonderful choices for shady spots; others do better in sun; and still others tolerate several different sets of conditions. Some prefer acid soils and do well under evergreens; many *are* evergreens. Others like their soil sweeter. Some grow better in damp areas, others in dry locales. There are tall plants that are also available as low growers, such as phlox and juniper. For dark spots where little else will grow, plant a shade-loving evergreen ground cover and be patient. Once it fills in, it will become a dense mat of leaves—variegated or all green.

A stretch of ground cover enriches a landscape, making a property look classier and neater than lawn ever could. It provides texture and interest and lends a sense of permanence to the design. Best of all, ground covers are easy to plant and generally require very little care—just a little weeding when intrepid interlopers elbow their way through the thick nap of stems.

Alas, even after they mature, ground covers may not be as showy as a perennial border, a rose garden, or a bed of bright annuals; but they are dependable, durable, and attractive, and you won't have to mow them. After a while you won't have to weed either; at least not much.

The key to getting ground covers established so they fill a space in a year or two rather than in five years is to plant them closer together than recommended—which takes more plants, and therefore more time and money, of course—or, in some cases, to begin with bigger "plugs" of the plants. At first, you'll still have some space between plants, so to help your ground covers grow into an attractive, dense display more quickly, fertilize according to your soil type and recommendations for the specific plants you choose, and keep out weeds with a thick layer of compost or mulch.

Except for the aforementioned invasives, there's really no such thing as a bad ground cover; but since different ground covers thrive in different conditions, it's a good idea to check the tags or ask questions.

Sometimes plants that aren't usually referred to as ground covers can do the same work. If many of one kind of perennial are massed together with little space between, they can prevent weeds and slow the loss of water. Hardy geraniums or coreopsis are good choices. Daylilies, lily of the valley, and irises also tend to form a solid mat that all but the most persistent weeds have a hard time breaching.

My favorite ground covers:

- **Corydalis** is a yellow, daisylike flower that spreads and softens the look of stone and paving.

- **Lamium** comes in attractive variegated or green-leaved species with tiny pink or yellow flowers. In some gardens, these plants tend to be a bit too vigorous. One catalogue describes them as "rampant-growing."

- **Lily of the valley** (*Convallaria*) makes a fine and fragrant ground cover. If you can bear to cut them, the stems and leaves look great in dainty bouquets.

- **Pachysandra** offers up tiny plumes of white flowers in a cluster of shiny evergreen leaves. This is a great choice for shady spots—even under shrubs and trees. It can be grown in sun, but then its usually dark-green leaves lighten to what I think is a less attractive yellow-green color. Try pachysandra with var-

the spare-time gardener

iegated leaves for an interesting effect.

- **Periwinkle** (*Vinca minor*), which even has a color named after its beautiful blue-purple flowers, has glossy evergreen leaves.
- In Maine, Bruce Riddell, ASLA, a colleague and favorite landscape architect, uses **blueberry turf** as a beautiful and effective ground cover for sunny spots. The fall color is spectacular.
- **Bunchberry,** which often grows wild and is extremely hardy, is a charming plant that grows low to the ground and spreads out nicely in shady areas. This member of the dogwood family proves the point through its white flowers and red berries that resemble those of its larger relatives.
- **Lilyturf** (*Liriope*), which creates an intriguing expanse of small, low mounds, makes an excellent, bright-green ground cover. Its flat leaves look something like grass but are tamer in that they never need mowing. Its blue or violet flower spikes add color.
- **Wooly thyme** (*Thymus*), sometimes called creeping thyme, is a decorative and delightfully scented way to fill in narrow spaces around paving stones and, on my walkway, where bricks meet granite edging at an odd angle.

WILDFLOWERS

The term *wildflower* leads us to a murky gray area. Many of the cultivated flowers we enjoy in our gardens today are really just wildflowers dressed up for a party. Their showy looks conceal their humble beginnings. In addition, there's the blurry line between weed and wildflower. If you enjoy a flowering plant in the wild, it's a wildflower; if it's trashy looking and is taking over its neighbors' turf, it's a weed.

Some wildflowers, lady's slipper orchids for instance, may be spectacular but don't take well to transplanting. Although the rules differ from state to state, it's illegal to pick or dig up some wildflowers. Why not let them be? That way everyone can enjoy them.

If you truly want to grow wildflowers, though, go to one of the nurseries that specializes in them. You may have to go online or order through a catalogue for the rarer species. I have few true wildflowers now, but here are a few favorites from present and past gardens:

- **Jack-in-the-pulpit** (*Arisaema triphyllum*) shoots up every spring under tall trees in my garden. The name says it all; use your imagination and you'll see that its flower looks like a person in a hooded pulpit. Later in the season, the brown-and-green flower is replaced by a tight cluster of red berries.

- **Dutchman's breeches** (*Dicentra cucullaria*) is my hands-down, all-time favorite. This relative of the bleeding heart (you can tell by the genus name *Dicentra*) has puffy, white flowers that do, indeed, look like old-fashioned pantaloons. The finely divided leaves add grace to the overall effect of this delightful little plant.

- **Virginia bluebell** (*Mertensia virginica*) grew profusely in my creek-side garden in Pennsylvania, along with trout lily, Dutchman's-breeches, and other dependable, yet delicate-looking, wildflowers. In a breeze, the bluebells' pendulous flowers created a haze of blue and purple in motion.

- **May apple** (*Podophyllum peltatum*) is new to my yard, but I'm looking forward to seeing it pop up and spread in my so-called woodland garden, where I planted several last year. Their broad, deeply lobed leaves start out folded in pleats and then form a mat of foliage parallel to the ground.

HERBS

Comparing fresh-picked herbs to what you find at the supermarket, whether dried in jars and cans or "fresh" in little cellophane packages, is like . . . well,

there's simply no comparison. They are entirely different animals—or vegetables, if you will.

Two words of caution, though: Unless you want to go into the pesto business or rival the gardens at Versailles, *think small.* Pots or tiny patches of garden can hold a great many different kinds of herbs, or a lot of just a few kinds if you prefer.

I like to mix several herb plants in a big basket, using a plastic liner filled with soilless mix or sterilized soil (don't forget the drainage holes). It only takes a few minutes to plant, and I can snip fresh herbs from the display all season. Depending on the basket, it either weathers beautifully over the summer or falls to pieces. Baskets are inexpensive, and the effect is charming, so it's worth losing a basket or two. Those baskets that survive are invited inside for the winter—after I rid them of any hitchhikers first, of course. On a sunny windowsill with an underliner to hold drips, this little garden provides fresh herbs all winter.

Thinking small doesn't mean you shouldn't *buy* big. I like to purchase hefty and healthy herb plants at the beginning of the season and stuff a bunch of them in pots and window boxes, as well as in baskets, near the front and kitchen doors. Their textures and subtle colors are lovely, and the scents as you or light breezes brush by them is amazing. Beginning with larger-sized

the spare-time gardener

plants means you can snip off branches liberally right from the start and still have plenty more to come.

Cutting herbs actually helps them become bushier and prevents them from bolting, or going to seed. Once that happens, the herbs (or other vegetables) sometimes become bitter, and the texture changes for the worse.

Some herbs are perennials, even in the far north. Since they seldom winter over in containers, these herbs should be planted in the ground, at least towards the end of the season. Beware of aggressive perennial herbs, though. Mint, for example, shows up every spring as tiny, delicate shoots and then quickly tries its best to choke out everything around it. We make a lot of mint-sprigged iced tea and tabouleh, which uses a good bit of it; but I make it a point to pull out any stalks that come up right among the ornamentals. Fortunately, they come out easily, roots and all.

BULBS THAT BLOOM IN THE SPRING—TRA-LA

The simple act of planting bulbs in the fall for spring bloom is a sign of hope, and merely the anticipation of a garden full of color can get us through many a cold, gray day. Winter aconite and snowdrops are willing to push their way through the snow to provide a touch of spring. Crocuses, hyacinths and grape hyacinths, anemones, daffodils (i.e., narcissus), and tulips aren't far behind and are favorites for good reason. Star of Bethlehem and other lesser-known bulbs are lovely and provide a broader range of color and bloom time. Plant as many bulbs as you can; you'll be rewarded for your time and trouble for many years to come.

Bulbs have their own powerhouses of nutrients within them. Although most like to grow in the sun, planting spring-flowering bulbs under deciduous trees is usually a safe bet. By the time the trees leaf out, the bulbs have bloomed.

While many other types of bulbs will thrive and multiply almost indefinitely, unfortunately most tulips last only a season or two before their vigor begins to wane. They're so spectacular, though, that many of us are willing to replant a batch every couple of years. Growers have developed hardier varieties, too; so don't neglect this plant entirely or you could be missing out on some incredible color in the spring garden.

VINES

These can be annual or perennial, deciduous or evergreen. They can serve as ground covers or grow up trellises and supports, or they can be used to camouflage eyesores in your yard or in your view. They can flower or not, and if they flower, they can be every color of the rainbow and every shade in between.

- **Trumpet vine** (*Campsis*) attracts hummingbirds and has small, shiny, nicely shaped leaves. It has a reputation as an invasive, but the stems can be pruned to keep it from getting out of hand. I'd be happier if my yellow trumpet vine were a little less reticent and a bit more rambunctious, but it does return each spring—just after I've pretty much decided it's given up the ghost.
- **Clematis** is an extraordinary perennial vine that bursts forth in a nearly solid wall of pinks, whites, and purples. The huge flowers have a tropical look that belies their hardiness. There are autumn-blooming clematis varieties, as well as those that bloom in high summer. One of my clematis plants came from Wave Hill and is not a vine at all, but rather sends up a clump of foot-high stems that bear blue, bell-shaped flowers. Many clematis vines are inexpensive, and they don't need much care. Why not try on a few for size? If you do, provide something on which they can grow (a trellis, fence, or even a tall tree), keep their "feet" cool while the rest of the plant gets

plenty of sun—easily accomplished by planting annuals around their base, and prune just once each year. Read *and save* the plant label, since the timing of pruning varies by species.
- **Ivy** (*Hedera helix*) is beautiful and classic, although some ivy can wreak havoc on masonry.
- **Morning glory** (*Ipomoea*) is a charming and easy annual vine for training up trellises and fences. It fills in quickly with heart-shaped foliage punctuated with glorious blue, white, and lavender blooms that look just like a miniature Georgia O'Keefe painting.
- **Sweet pea** (*Lathyrus odoratus*), another annual, is equally charming and has the added attraction of a lovely scent.

ANNUALS—WORTH IT EVERY TIME

Plants that last just one season, called annuals, may not seem worth the time you spend choosing them, planting them, and caring for them. But once you see what they can do to brighten and beautify a garden with color and texture, you'll probably decide it's worth the effort to include them each year. Annuals are generally inexpensive, and many are easily sown from seed if you're so inclined.

Again, plants that are considered hardy only in more southern climes can usually be grown as annuals in the north. If you pay attention to the zone map, you won't be disappointed; and you can consider it a real gift if the plant survives through the winter.

Some annuals offer another bonus: They renew themselves each year by dropping seeds that winter over to sprout wherever they fall. Watching these "volunteers" appear is a delightful part of gardening. Besides, waiting to see what they become gives us a reason to delay weeding—as if we really need an excuse!

Unlike choosing perennials, where you may want to stay with tried-and-true favorites, planting annuals offers you a safe opportunity to experiment with new plants, colors, sizes, and other variables to add interest and texture to your garden. Who knows, you may like the effect so much it will change your ideas about the overall color palette with which you paint your landscape.

pers can do well in partial shade, too; but don't expect as much in the way of blooms.

When I'm in the mood for orange and yellow, I plant dwarf marigold and nasturtium. I plant multihued portulaca, snapdragon, and nicotiana for sentimental reasons.

I love the brilliant and unusual colors of dusky-centered osteospermum; the clear pinks and bright whites of cosmos; and the familiar, lipstick-red flowers of geranium (*Pelargonium*). This is the red, white, pink, or purple "geranium" we so often grow in containers or plant in the garden. I detect a certain sneer in serious gardeners' attitude towards these geraniums, but I can't fathom why. This is a plant that comes in vibrant colors, has leaves in a wide variety of shapes and even scents, stands up to wind and heavy rain, produces upright and hanging varieties, and blooms all summer and well into fall if you take a moment every couple of days to snap off the old flowers.

ANNUALS FOR SUN

If your garden has six to eight hours of sun a day and fairly decent soil, you can successfully grow hundreds of different flowering annuals. These range from tiny-blossomed specialty petunias that are great in hanging baskets, to tall and showy cut flowers like gladiolus, zinnia, and canna. Some of these sun worship-

ANNUALS FOR SHADE

So many perennials thrive and provide bright flowers in the shade that it's often easier to use them in the darker parts of the garden than it is to use annuals. Nonetheless, it's fun to add the still-brighter dash of color that annuals can bring to shady or partially shady spots.

Every year, I pin a lot of my hopes on impatiens; and it hasn't let me down yet. While its spikes of miniscule flowers aren't much to behold, coleus is another shade-tolerant plant that can be very attractive. Its serrated, brilliantly veined leaves come in every shade of red, from pink to burgundy, and of green, from chartreuse to forest. Annual begonia does fine in shade or sun and comes primarily in pink, red, and white. The leaves offer variety, too.

AN ANNUAL BY ANY OTHER NAME

There's a word being bandied about: temperennials. These plants are not perennial in the more-northern zones in the U.S. Instead they're tender bulbs or tropicals that have to be treated as annuals in many areas. Nonetheless, they add so much to the garden through their colors and shapes that a lot of gardeners plant them, hardiness be damned.

Vendors consider many of these specimens choice, and they price them accordingly. That's not to say you shouldn't buy them; but if price is a consideration, you might want to see if you can winter them over indoors (dahlias, for example) or find other plants that fit the bill.

THE WOODLAND GARDEN

If you're trying to grow grass or sun-loving annuals or perennials under trees, you might have noticed that they don't want to be there. They sulk and mope along and generally fail to thrive. Why coddle them? Who has the time?

Why not put in some ferns and hostas, bleeding hearts, hellebores, or other shade-loving perennials? And be sure to add some bulbs that bloom each spring before the trees leaf out so you'll have a display you can enjoy all through the season every year.

In our small yard, I have what I laughingly refer to as my woodland garden. It's basically a couple of big, old trees under which a carpet of violets thrives, and has probably thrived for a hundred or more years. When we moved in 15 years ago, there were also some columbine, Jack-in-the-pulpit, and monkshood. Over time, I've added hostas in various sizes and shades of green, a few ostrich ferns in the hope of harvesting enough fiddleheads for supper (alas . . . a feeble hope), bleeding hearts, rhododendrons, and astilbes—all shade lovers. A friend gave me a pot of snowdrops, which are not spreading wildly but do at least return each year to brighten the tangled roots of the tall fir tree at the center of this garden. I've learned since planting them that this soil and location are not a snowdrop's cup of tea.

The European ginger I purchased from a fancy catalogue many years ago finally gave up in last winter's extreme cold, so I replaced it with the hellebores. Last year, I planted three pots of variegated ornamental grasses in an area of my woodland garden that gets a little sun. We'll see.

The biggest gamble of all is a kousa dogwood I bought at Coastal Maine Botanical Gardens' annual plant sale. It's listing to starboard, a handy horticultural demonstration of where our prevailing winds are; so we'll wait and hope it survives.

I've also planted daffodils, tulips, grape hyacinths, and other bulbs, and we thoroughly enjoy these harbingers of spring. As small as this garden is, it gives me great joy. I groom a winding path that leads from the front walk towards the water, and when I get around to it, I plunk down some good-looking stepping stones I picked up on sale several years ago. I left some of the sizeable rocks I found while working in this area but made sure they remained mostly buried, so they look like they belong—because they *do* belong. They were there first.

My biggest mistake was transplanting some variegated aegopodium from one area of the yard, where it was safely contained, to the woodland garden. I thought the touch of white on the leaves would lend vibrancy to the shade. It was vibrant all right; this vicious plant threatened to take over. Friends in the know tell me I'll never really be rid of it until I dig out all the soil and start fresh. No way! I'm not going to mess up

my entire garden to atone for one well-meaning mistake. I'll just keep pulling up those little suckers as they appear—before they know what hits them.

That experience is my best argument for avoiding invasive species, many of which are sold in garden centers or through catalogues. It's unbelievable how many invasives are peddled to unsuspecting gardeners. If a plant tag reads "vigorous" or "aggressive," leave that plant where you found it—at the nursery!

It sounds as though I spend an inordinate amount of time in this small, shady garden, but (except for the aegopodium episode) I don't. It looks how it looks, and whatever's in bloom at a particular time is my pride and joy. Visitors and the neighbors seem to like it, and it beats boring, struggling, not-so-green grass hands down.

TREES

If you've decided you want a tree and you've chosen a spot for it, there's more to consider before you get out your wallet. A tree is not only a bigger investment than a lot of other plants; it's also just plain bigger. Make sure it fits in with your landscape plan, not so much because of the size it is when you buy it, but because of the size it will be when it's mature.

Do you want an evergreen or a deciduous tree? Or maybe you want a larch, which is a conifer that loses its needles in a brilliant show of gold each fall and returns to life at winter's end with a brilliant spring green hue.

Do you want a tree with a columnar, upright habit, or one that spreads its branches out and then out some more? Perhaps you'd like to plant a graceful, weeping tree—a cherry with lovely spring blossoms, a Japanese maple, or an Atlas cedar. These can create dramatic statements.

If you'd like a flowering tree, decide whether you want the fruit to be edible or if you want the tree for strictly ornamental purposes. If you want to enjoy the fruit, look for plants that are nearly care free, rather than those that require the use of pesticides and more

special care than you're willing to give them before they can bear fruit suitable for your table.

In addition to tall fir trees with shallow roots, we have big old Norway maples, my new kousa dogwood, a messy alder, and an ancient, gnarly crabapple tree. If the latter ever kicks the bucket, I'm going to replace it with a yellow magnolia that's good and hardy, or maybe a stand of white birch trees or a dawn redwood. Now there's a lovely tree! It was thought to be extinct, but now it's back with a vengeance. If I had more than a little land, I'd plant a larch grove because of that tree's grace and beauty (and of course as a nod to Monty Python—"Number One: The Larch").

the spare-time gardener

22

the honest bribe

There's nothing wrong with being sybaritic. After all, what's the point of having a garden if you can't and don't enjoy it? You want to hang out in your hammock. Frolic in the grass. Barbeque for the masses. Party hearty. Don't you? Of course you do.

But it's hard to be sybaritic when your face and hands are full of grimy soil and sweat. To get the garden of even your most humble dreams, and do it without an aching back and calloused hands and knees, you need help. And better yet, help you can get for free—or nearly free. Besides, everything's more fun if you have company doing it.

Enlist your friends and neighbors, your kids and spouse if you have them, your co-workers—anyone you can entice into your garden. It's the enticing part that's dicey, you say. Not at all. Everyone has a price; you just have to find out what that price is. Remember

that there's no dishonor in an honest bribe.

THE TOM SAWYER APPROACH

We're not advocating trickery here. Just put on your broadest, most convincing smile, and tell your intended "victims" how much you love working in your garden. Tell them what great exercise it is and how many calories gardening burns (hundreds each hour!), and you'll be telling the absolute truth.

You'll recall that this is how Tom Sawyer got his pals to whitewash that fence. Now, go Tom one better. Suggest that in return for help with garden chores (specified or unspecified), you will provide the aforementioned barbeque, a glass of wine or a frosty drink, a great DVD movie, a board or video game, a swim in the pool, a poker party, a shared shopping spree . . . whatever. You know your audience and can frame your offer (bribe) accordingly.

You'll be surprised at how many people will jump at the chance to dig in the dirt, especially if they're apartment or condo dwellers. If they have gardens of their own to tend, you might have to offer to help them in equal measure. If they're tyros in the garden, you might have to give them some instruction to get them started on the right path (you don't want anyone pulling out your clematis vines or other precious perennials that in spring might look for all the world like weeds).

By enlisting help, you'll save time and have fun. Your bribe is *probably* worth it, whatever the price.

23

gardener beware

Whoever came up with the now-cliché, "If it seems too good to be true, it probably is," might well have been a gardener. The majority of plants you'll buy or receive as gifts will grow well and add beauty to your garden and your life. There are some black sheep in every plant family, however, and these should be avoided, or at least contained.

DON'T INVITE INVASIVE PLANTS INTO YOUR GARDEN

Unless you want to spend more time digging up plants than planting them, avoid invasive species. Unfortunately, even reputable companies sometimes sell plants that have a tendency to overtake your garden, and what's tame in one area or zone can be a monster in another. In addition, plants you might love—some honeysuckles, roses, winterberry, barberry, and burning bush, to name a few—are considered invasive.

When reading descriptions on tags or in catalogues, watch out for buzz-words such as "aggressive," "vigorous," or even "fast-growing." One catalogue pointed out that under the right conditions monarda (bee balm) is "vigorous to the point of invasiveness, perhaps past it." This kind of forthright terminology should raise red flags for you.

Sometimes the descriptions offer rave reviews of plants that can invade our gardens. Aegopodium (bishop's weed) and winterberry are still being sold, and we can only hope that the selections are less "vigorous" than those promoted in the past.

BEWARE OF FRIENDS BEARING GIFTS

By accepting transplants from other gardeners, you may unwittingly be introducing a plant into your garden that's behaved like a runaway train in their own. Ask a question or two about how the shared plants grow best, and listen carefully to the answers. By reading between the lines, you can find out if, indeed, they grow *too* well.

If that's the case, and you like the looks of the plant and want to accept the gift, simply grow it in a container or in a spot where it can't encroach on other plants' space.

Sharing plants with friends is one of the nicest and most neighborly ways to show you care and of acknowledging a shared pastime or passion. As your garden thrives and your plants multi- ply, be sure to return the favor with good healthy specimens from your own garden.

DON'T PICK UP HITCHHIKERS OR DERELICTS

Before adding a plant to your wagon at the nursery, or before planting those you've accepted from friends, give these new additions to your landscape a thorough going-over. Bugs could be tagging along for the ride. Diseases could be lurking. Weeds could be nestling amidst the stems.

Look for healthy, well-formed, insect-free leaves and stems. If they're misshapen or badly wilted, tattered or chewed, discolored or leggy, beware; danger this way lies.

24

your planting plan—exercise 6

You have a general idea of where you want new and existing plants in your landscape. Now it's time to decide where you want specific plants to grow. This goes hand in hand with choosing and then purchasing the plants.

On a new tracing-paper overlay on top of the landscape plan you created in Exercise 5—or, better yet, on a photocopy of your plan—you'll indicate where you want individual specimens or patches of plants to fill up the garden areas you've developed.

You can do this for each season if you'll have plantings that are at their best at different times—spring bulbs, summer flowers, and fall favorites in what are called sequential plantings. Planting with the full season in mind is a great way to keep your garden in bloom, but let's just start with a planting plan for summer.

But not yet. First, you'll take the time to find out about plants, reconnoiter at the garden center, and make a list of those that will work in your garden and that you'd like to include (see below). Then, when you're ready, you'll take the list of plants and assign a letter to each of the different kinds.

When they're numbered, using your landscape plan as a guide and your tracing paper or photocopy as a worksheet, you'll mark off areas where you want the plants on your list. To accomplish this, use circles or whatever shape fits the area to be occupied by a plant species, and then write in the letter of the type of plant you want in that area. Using colored pencils to show bloom shades in each area is fun and helpful.

You don't need a circle for each individual plant—just each kind (example: A = impatiens, B = dwarf marigold, C = giant marigold, D = pachysandra).

PLANTING PLAN— EXERCISE #6

THE PLANTS

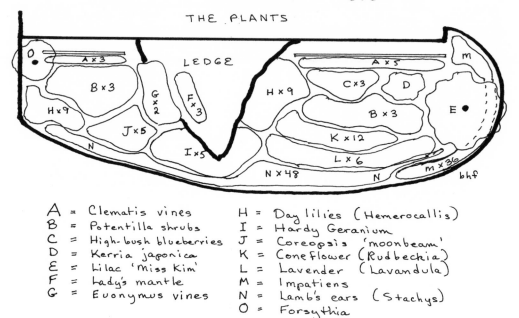

A = Clematis vines
B = Potentilla shrubs
C = High-bush blueberries
D = Kerria japonica
E = Lilac 'Miss Kim'
F = Lady's mantle
G = Evonymus vines

H = Day lilies (Hemerocallis)
I = Hardy Geranium
J = Coreopsis 'moonbeam'
K = Coneflower (Rudbechia)
L = Lavender (Lavandula)
M = Impatiens
N = Lamb's ears (Stachys)
O = Forsythia

You might have only one letter in an entire flower bed, meaning that it will be filled with just one type of plant; or you might have dozens of circles, each with its own letter, meaning the bed will be filled with a lot of different kinds of plants. You can have circles within circles—a specimen plant surrounded by ground cover, say. A letter may be repeated all over your property if it indicates a plant you want to have in many areas.

Finally, using information you've gleaned at the garden center, you'll estimate how many plants of each kind you'll need. Then you'll go shopping and plant the plants and grow the plants and keep track of the plants—and do it all over again next year.

But not yet . . .

DECISIONS, DECISIONS

George W. Perkins, my husband's grandfather, who was a friend and cohort of Theodore Roosevelt's and a partner of J.P. Morgan's, had a philosophy about making choices and a saying to go with it: "Do not seem to pick or choose, but with a quick and ready eye select the best." It's become my shopping mantra and has saved me countless hours of picking and choosing. But, it only works if you already have a pretty good idea what you're looking for.

Take a nursery, a.k.a. garden center, for example. Presented with row upon row of plant pulchritude and a cacophony of color—the mainstays of any nursery worth its *Salvia superba*—how on earth can you decide which plants you want to put in the little red wagons (or

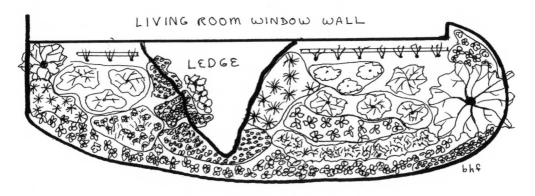

LIVING ROOM WINDOW WALL

LEDGE

LAWN

Your planting plan

other conveyances) customers use to make their selections? Which ones are worth your hard-earned cash? Which ones do you want to take home and nurture, sometimes for years and years?

Just as important: Which ones aren't going to take all the time you have? Moreover, how can you actually *make* all these choices without wasting a lot of time?

The answer? Again, you have to spend some time to make time *and* good decisions. Besides, this won't take as much time as you imagine—and you'll like the results.

RECONNAISSANCE

Before you ever get anywhere near the little red wagon or the cash register, you should first reconnoiter. A trip to a couple of nurseries within striking distance of your home will yield information and will ultimately save time. By simply browsing, reading tags, and asking questions, you'll get ideas, a feel for

prices, and a sense of what's out there—both in plants and accessories.

Take notes. Jot down the recommended spacing of plants you like and the conditions *they* like. For flowering plants, notice the bloom times. This information should be on the tags; if not, feel free to ask the nursery staff. It's their job to make sure you make the right decision; after all, they want you to be a steady customer for the right reasons, not because you're forever replacing plants that have failed. Doing your homework before you ever pull out your wallet is time well spent and money well saved.

SAFE AT HOME—MAKE A PLANT LIST

Now that you know your options, retreat to the safety of your home, that is, nowhere in sight of a cash register or red wagon, and follow these steps:

- Referring to the notes you've made at the nursery, make a list of plants for the parts of your garden you want to plant right now. Be specific, but be aware that you may have to substitute A for B—so have a fallback plan.

- Also make a shopping list. Include a few bags each (or more if you're sure you'll need them) of mulch and compost and a container of fertilizer, if you don't already have some at home. If you run out, you can buy more bags; just don't start with too many.
- Take an inventory of your tools and add to your shopping list any that are broken or missing so you can replace them.

Remember to let the landscape plan drive the plant selections that go on your list. As we're told with grocery shopping, if it isn't on your list, don't buy it. It's easy to fall madly in love with a plant at the nursery. You'll be tempted to bring it home, thinking you'll find the perfect place for it— somewhere. 'Twas not always thus. More often than not, out of desperation, you end up planting it (heeling it in) somewhere that doesn't really suit it, "just for the time being." You never do find the right spot for it, so then it either dies, making you feel bad, or struggles along, making you feel almost as bad, and reminding you forevermore of your mistake.

Believe me, I speak from experience. There was this $70 bargain kousa dogwood, poor thing, slightly lopsided but I just had to have it . . . but that's another story.

When you've completed your planting plan and your plant shopping list, put the list under your pillow—and sleep on it. By morning, you may have changed your mind about this or that. Change your list accordingly.

START WITH YOUR LANDSCAPE PLAN— AND THINK

Before you can create a planting plan based on the garden areas you developed in your landscape plan, you need to narrow down the list of millions of available plants to the ones you want in your garden. I know, I know—there's so little time and so much to grow. Give it some thought.

Think Height

Even if you hadn't heard it before, you already know intuitively that taller plants should go in the back of a flower bed or landscape, with gradually smaller plants towards the front. After all, you want to be able to see every single plant; otherwise, why bother?

If the bed follows the line of a building, wall, or fence, plant the taller materials closer to the structure. If you see a bed from all sides, then put tall

the spare-time gardener

plants in the center, and surround them with progressively shorter plants.

Think Size

You've surely seen homes dwarfed by massive evergreens looming over them. You might live in one of these homes. The plants, usually evergreen shrubs, were probably purchased years before and grew and grew and grew, much to everyone's delight at first, and now to the owners' chagrin. Some shrubs will readily produce new shoots if you cut them back, while with others, if you cut off the top layer of green you're left with an unsightly brown mess.

To avoid choosing shrubs and trees that will cause problems down the road, before you make a purchase, ask or check the tag to find out how big they'll eventually become. Remember that a "dwarf" plant is not necessarily always going to be smaller than its big brothers; it just might take it longer to reach its ultimate size. In addition, check on pruning practices for a particular plant.

Of course, while slow growth is fine, even desirable, in some situations, in other areas you might want to make a big splash, and soon. Here again, check the tag and ask the experts.

Think Ahead

Plants should never be allowed to grow too close to a house. Allow space for maintenance—room for you or people you hire to paint, repoint brick, wash windows, or whatever else might be necessary next year, or ten years from now. Wouldn't it be a shame, and a duplication of effort, to have to pull out your plants (and then replant them) so a painter can reach your clapboard?

Plants and buildings need to breathe, too, so maintain air circulation between plants and your house. Remember, too, that security is an issue if you have big bushes hiding doorways and walkways.

You should also take into account the drip line from the roof. What a waste of time it would be to create a display and then effectively drown your plants. Again, planting away from the house allows access for painting or maintenance.

If you're planting by an openwork fence, picket for example, it's fun and easy to create a cottage garden effect by allowing flowers in an array of heights and hues to tumble through the fencing. Think carefully, though, before you plant close to that fence. If it's made of natural wood or plastic, that shouldn't be a problem. If it will eventually require a new coat of paint, you'd better stick with annuals, or you'll be in a pickle come painting time.

Think Color and Continuity

Now's the time to concentrate on the colors you want around you throughout the growing season, and beyond.

How they're combined is every bit as important as the colors you choose. The one-of-each garden may have its charms, but for the greatest effect with the least effort, plant in swaths of color. Even in a large garden, as you transition from one color to another, proceed gently, easing from one shade to the next.

Some gardeners like the look of a monochromatic garden—a "white garden" or a "blue garden" or a "red garden," they'll call it. Of course, there are many shades of blue or red, or even white; and zeroing in on one or another color can simplify your planning by narrowing down your choices. While you're planning, though, remember that no matter what hue you choose, there will always be plenty of green in the mix. Foliage, after all, goes hand in hand with flowers. So as you picture this garden in your mind's eye, factor in the greenery.

As appealingly simple as the idea may be, you probably won't want to be so single-minded as to limit yourself to one shade, and one shade only, throughout your entire landscape. You'll want to experiment with color and include favorite plants, no matter what their color.

The garden is not the place where you want too many complementary colors cheek by jowl. Remember the color wheel from high school art classes? Using neighboring colors in neighboring plants creates a gentle flow. On the other hand, complementary colors— orange and blue, red and green, yellow and purple—are extreme opposites. They feel active; they bounce off each other. It's fun to add a splash of contrasting color in the garden, but use restraint if you don't want the overall effect to be less than pleasing. The eye, and the mind, enjoy continuity.

That said, I believe *all* colors look good on plants. That bilious shade of chartreuse may make Aunt Adelaide look seasick, but it's delicate and charming in bells of Ireland, lady's-mantle, and hellebores. A fiery fuchsia might take away your appetite if used on your dining room walls, but in a phlox or a geranium—or indeed a fuchsia—it's delightful.

Your choice of color does have an effect on the overall mood of your garden, though. Back to high school art: Warm colors (red, yellow, orange) create a vibrant, lively atmosphere in your garden, while their cool counterparts (blue, green, violet) can chill down the feel of a sweltering day.

The darkness or lightness of the hue is called its *value*, and this can also affect your perception. Using plants with dark flowers or foliage, and there are some stunning options, can create a dramatic effect. These work well as accent plants. Choosing primarily lighter hues will provide a more soothing atmosphere.

the spare-time gardener

While adding a container or a pocket of dark plants and foliage can create a stunning counterpoint to medium hues, juxtaposing the extremes—the dramatically dark alongside the paler, gentler light—can be jarring and make the lighter hues look washed out. Tread softy, but be comforted by the thought that if you don't like a plant where it is, you can always dig it up and put it somewhere else.

In addition to grouping plants by color, plant several (or better yet, a lot) of a single plant in one location to maximize the effect—and minimize the effort. You can fill your garden with a lot of plant material, but it doesn't have to contain a lot of different *kinds* of plants.

Think Natural; Think Native

Plants that are native to your area are workhorses that can withstand all the weather your zone can dish out without faltering. To make your gardening life easier, and add attractive flowers and foliage at the same time, try to incorporate some into your planting plan.

Woody plants or shrubs add a naturalistic feel to your garden. They come in all sizes and habits, and as long as they're kept in scale with the rest of your plantings, they look great in a mixed border.

Think Longevity

Why spend your precious time planting flowers that bloom for a week and then wither and look pathetic for the rest of the season—or worse still, have to be dug out and tossed away? Why spend half your summer looking at a sea of green with hardly a bloom in sight?

There are flowering plants that "specialize" in blooming at various times throughout the year, except in the deepest winter. There are species that produce flowers very early or later in spring, early or late in summer, and well into fall. If you start with the earliest spring bulbs and end with late-fall chrysanthemums, you'll have many months of color in the garden.

In addition, numerous annuals and perennials will bloom from one month to another with super-long, season-spanning displays; these are your best friends in the garden.

Within species, there are varieties that bloom at different times. Take daffodils, for example: Some flower while others are just popping through the ground. Use this to your advantage and create a show of color that lasts for a month instead of a week.

Before giving a plant a home, therefore, find out when it blooms and for how long. With the endless number of selections out there, and the difference from zone to zone, it's impossible to generalize. Check this information on each plant tag or with the nursery staff. If you plan your garden so adjacent plants bloom in succession, with plenty of time overlap, you'll be rewarded with continuous color throughout the growing season.

Another advantage of interspersing plants that bloom at different times is that newly emerging plants and blooms will camouflage the withering foliage of plants that are dying back (spring bulbs, for example) before these early beauties disappear entirely. The successive flowering will keep your garden bright.

Think Snow

What about that fourth season? Once you tidy up your garden in the fall, you can either be left with a bare expanse of brown (or white) where your gardens were, or you can enjoy continued texture and color. Winter can be long and dreary, so why not brighten it up with more than snow?

It's all in the planning. As you create your planting plan, think about adding interest to your winter landscape. This can be done with texture, color, and shape. Evergreen conifers and broadleaved evergreens such as rhododendron provide texture and rich color (green, that is). You can plant shrubs and trees that possess interesting and colorful bark and shapes (birch and red-twig dogwood for color; Harry Lauder's walking stick for oddly convoluted branches). Witch hazel offers brilliant yellow flowers when little else will bloom. If you plant holly and other shrubs that produce bright berries, the birds will love you for it.

And then at winter's end, if you've planned well, winter aconite, snowdrop, hellebore, and other exceptionally early-blooming plants will arrive—and just in time, too.

Think Low Maintenance

There are no bad plants—well, hardly any. There are just plants that are wrong for the conditions you can give them. Before you bring a plant home, it saves time to know what it will ask of you, and what you can give it in return.

Here's where a little homework at the garden center comes in handy. Read the tags; ask the staff; look it up. However you proceed, you'll need to know some things about each kind of plant you want to put in your garden.

With so many variables to consider, it makes sense and saves time to plant fewer species of plants.

If you don't want to create a lot of extra work for yourself (and who does?), consider the following:

- Is it easy to grow, OR is it a temperamental diva?
- Is it resistant to pests and diseases, OR will it attract them?

- Is it a fast grower, OR will it take its time (you may want some of each, depending on your garden)?
- Does it need regular pruning or daily deadheading, OR will it thrive without all that attention?
- Is it sturdy enough to withstand a stiff breeze, OR does it need to be staked and tied to protect it from the slightest zephyr?
- Will it tolerate the moisture conditions where you live, OR will it need constant watering or can't stand to have its feet wet?
- Will it thrive in the sun (or shade), OR will it need more (or less) light than I can give it?
- Can I disguise its spent foliage with other plants, OR will it look simply dreadful?
- Is it too picky about the soil it likes, OR will it do well where I want to plant it?

Think Containers

Planting in pots, boxes, urns, old boots, or other containers is an easy way to get the most impact from your plants. These mini gardens can be filled with small shrubs, flowering or foliage plants, herbs and vegetables—or all of the above.

As you learned in "Plant Me Now," your earlier foray into planting a single splashy container, using plenty of plant material creates the greatest effect. Otherwise, your container garden will look thin and wan rather than robust.

Your plants are primarily green with bright spots of color provided by the blossoms. Pots and planters can either add more color or they can add atmosphere, or they can serve both purposes.

Try to select plants that will offer extended bloom and have complementary colors and textures. That doesn't mean they should be the same; they should simply look great together. You'll know them when you see them.

Think New—Or Not

Should you go with the tried and true, or try something new? There's a lot to be said for the comfort level old favorites can offer, but gardening is all about imagination and experimentation. So by all means, try that spectacular plant you've seen in a magazine or catalogue—just don't create a garden full of experiments. You'll get a polka-dot effect, and in some cases those dots will be empty because a plant just didn't suit its space.

25

gnomes we've known and loved— furnishing and ornamenting the garden

Just as plants go in and out of fashion, so too do lawn ornaments and garden structures. Gazing balls gave way to gnomes. When gnomes fell off their pedestals, it was time for the wind chime to take over. Scallop-edged, inside-out truck tires and plastic flamingoes will probably always be with us; gazing balls have bounced back; and the gnomes seem to have returned from wherever they've been "holing up" for the past 20 years (maybe due to the influence of that delightful French movie, *Amelie*).

For years, practically every garden center has set aside some of its sales space for concrete critters, stone statuary, plastic pretties, and wooden whatsits. Now there are

new entries in the field: Fiberglass, resin, and stone composites that look for all the world like real concrete, terra-cotta, ceramic, or stone are used to make everything from reclining frogs to rococo fountains. Even though purists (I'm one, but conversion is under way) might object that these imposters are not the real thing, these new materials make garden objects a darned

the spare-time gardener

sight easier to carry and move. They're sometimes sturdy enough to be left out through the winter, too, although they look rather forlorn covered in snow.

Different kinds of furnishings also have their day. Metal gliders and chairs with decoratively perforated seats went out of style; now they're back. Wooden benches are in, and granite is taking hold, at least with those who can afford it. The molded plastic stacking chair and lounge chair seem to be edging ahead of the webbed, metal-framed folding versions, except maybe at the beach. Umbrellas that were once striped-canvas, hexagonal affairs are now flexible and come in a raft of shapes, sizes, and patterns.

FORM FOLLOWING FUNCTION

Of course, some ornamental objects can be both decorative and practical; and garden furniture is useful, if not always practical. Containers of every shape, size, color, and texture can hold plants. If installed well, even the most beautiful stepping stones can provide firm footing through a garden while helping to preserve the plants around them.

Trellises, arbors, shelves, and brackets are often extremely decorative but, at the same time, can be essential for growing and displaying your plants. Fountains can double as birdbaths or

pet watering holes. We have a colorful wind sock at the end of our dock that's far better at indicating wind speed and direction than the little electronic gizmo on our living room wall.

Using furniture outside extends your living and dining space so you can enjoy the great outdoors when the weather is fine. If the conditions are right, there's very little that can match the pleasure of relaxing, alone or with family and friends, in your own yard. Umbrellas, awnings, and canopies provide shade. Tables and chairs offer a warm-weather dining option.

If you have a covered porch, or better yet a screened porch, you can spend more time outdoors in warm weather; and you can get away with using more delicate materials. As a teenager, I often slept out on the wide second-floor porch of our house. Ocean breezes and the sunrise would wake me, and it felt wonderful. I'd do that now if I had a screened porch; the mosquitoes in Maine are hungrier and more tenacious than their predecessors in Cape May County, New Jersey.

Bird feeders, baths, and houses can be beautiful or utilitarian. No matter how they look, though, they can provide a great deal of enjoyment, and can help support the bird population. Spending just 10 or 15 minutes *really paying attention* to animals can do worlds for our understanding and mental outlook. Whether the subject of your attention is the birds that frequent your feeder, the squirrels that vie for the birds' food, or your own pets, try it; you'll be enthralled and enlightened.

LET THERE BE LIGHT

If you want to spend some of your evening time outdoors or accent special trees and architectural features, lighting is essential. Candles add a romantic glow, and some may even keep away the bugs; but sometimes you need the more intense light that only bulbs can provide.

Battery-operated and solar-powered fixtures are easier and quicker to move than their plugged-in, or wired-in, alternatives. Lights that work on batteries are really only an option as long as you choose rechargeable batteries or don't mind spending a lot on replacements. The advances in solar lighting mean they provide real illumination, rather than the sputtering, pale glow they previously offered—that is, if you have enough sun for them. There are solar versions of uplights, downlights, and spotlights. There are also solar candle lanterns, where the engineered flickering is an advantage.

It's time for a public service announcement from the folks at the International Dark-Sky Association, whose mantra is "Bring Back the Night Sky." Make sure lights point downwards or directly onto the object you want to illuminate, rather than send their light needlessly towards the sky. Pointing your light skyward without reason or using lights that have no shields over their tops will raise your bulb costs and electricity bills and contribute to the overall glow on our planet—not a good glow, as anyone who's tried to look at the stars from a city or the suburbs can tell you.

STRIKING A HAPPY BALANCE

It takes a lot of self-control to resist some of the appealing ornaments that fill gardening catalogues and are displayed prominently in stores. It's important to realize, though, that there's such a thing as too many ornaments, and even too much furniture, in the garden. It takes time to install and maintain it all; and after the number of structures and ornaments reaches a certain point, it can negatively affect the sense of tranquility your garden can offer. Your yard takes on that cluttered look.

The trick is in knowing when you've reached that point. Consider what purpose each object in your garden serves. If you want to avoid neighbors' unfriendly comments about the bright-bloomered cutouts tending your flower beds, or don't like cars screeching to a halt to snap photos of the flock of flamingoes or fairy ring of fake mushrooms you've planted on your front lawn, consider the following:

- Some ornaments are nothing but eye candy, which is not necessarily a bad thing. Just the same, if you're tempted to bring home just one more whirligig from the local craft fair or order that sundial from your favorite catalogue (and you already have a working wristwatch), think twice. Is it so cute or beautiful that you simply can't resist it? Where will you put it in the winter? Is it durable enough that it will survive without a lot of pampering? Will it be the straw that breaks the camel's back—ornamentally speaking?

- Utilitarian objects are easier to justify. Consistency is the key here. If you can find a unifying factor—choosing similar styles or selecting them or painting them all in one or two colors, for example—you might avoid a fragmented effect.

- Siting them correctly is important, too. If a trellis is plopped down in the middle of a lawn with no pathway leading to it or from it, and no plantings around it, it will look weird no matter how beautiful it is. If you want to insert a structure into your overall design, find just the right place. If there is no good place, then either make one or resist the temptation to include that particular object.

OUTDOOR DÉCOR FOR THE SPARE-TIME GARDENER

Covering and/or storing garden furniture is time consuming and has very little entertainment value; and replacing delicate lawn chairs every year isn't much fun either. Why not go the time-saving route? When shopping for outdoor furnishings, look for easy-care materials. Find items that won't rust and don't weigh a ton. Only buy them if you can clean them by turning a hose on them.

Although prices run the gamut from discount to astronomically high, for a reasonable price you can find good-looking furnishings that will last for many years without a lot of maintenance. Some Adirondack chairs that look perfectly fine are made of recycled plastic soda bottles and are impervious to the weather, while those made of wood often have high-tech finishes that keep them looking great. Wicker that needs painting or sealing every season has given way to year-round wicker with sturdy steel frames.

Ecologically sensible, sustainable woods are used for benches, chairs, and tables that can be left outside to weather naturally. Molded plastic chairs and tables come in colors and shapes to fit every taste and need, as well as every body. Many hammocks are now made of durable fabrics, and the stands will last forever.

Newer fabrics used in pillows, umbrellas, and awnings resist sun, rain, and extreme temperatures so you don't have to scurry to bring pillows indoors at the first sign of the slightest sprinkle. There's a complete spectrum of colors, patterns, and finishes.

WATER, WATER EVERYWHERE

Water features are wonderful; at least you'd think so. They come in a dizzying array of sizes, shapes, materials, and themes. Some set up in no time, and some even run on solar energy. No matter what their size, fountains and waterfalls can offer the soothing sound of moving water. You can use a fountain as a focal point, choosing various spouts or sculpted ornaments (frog, fish, heron, child) as the source of the stream. Adding stones and surrounding it with plants provides a natural look.

You can add a few small fish and aquatic plants to a mini pond and enjoy watching the goldfish circle amidst the lily pads. But beware—it's possible to run into some time-consuming problems, or even environmental or safety nightmares. Fountains and ponds, like fishbowls, need to be cleaned. Otherwise, you can experience nasty blooms of algae or other organisms. In some states (Maine, for one), it's illegal to introduce any nonnative fish into a home pond because they might skip over to a bigger water feature—a stream, lake, or ocean—while we're off our guard. Some aquatic plants are so invasive they're also illegal. If you use an indoor unit outside, you can face some electrical safety issues.

As with other elements of your garden, think carefully before you commit to purchasing and caring for a fountain or other water feature. Even the smallest fountain needs some maintenance, and keeping a pond healthy can be an overwhelming task.

If you have room for a pond or a large water garden, as well as the time to maintain it or the wherewithal to have someone else care for it, first consult the pros or, better still, let them build the feature for you. They'll be able to employ methods that result in a beautiful water garden and still combine ecology and economy; and that's to everyone's advantage.

On a lesser scale, if you have a covered or enclosed porch, setting up a ready-made tabletop fountain can provide pleasing sounds and a decorative accent. Since the maintenance required is minimal, you can get some of the effect of a water garden for a lot less trouble.

If you don't have a covered outdoor area, and can't see your way clear to installing a water feature outside, why not buy or make a fountain for inside the house? That way you can bring the outdoors in—a fine way to extend your garden.

26

let's go shopping

Now, finally, the last frost date is nearly here; and the weather forecast is for a string of warm, fair days. You've probably already decided which nursery or nurseries you want to patronize. Your choice should be based on your comfort level with the staff, the selections available, and—most important of all—the quality of the plant materials. While it might not be essential to purchase large, it is *imperative* to purchase healthy!

With your list of plants in hand, and your wallet handy, you can now return to your favorite garden center. And this time you mean business.

Again, try to pick a time when it won't be too busy. Empty your trunk or cargo area of the snow shovel and other winter detritus, and put down a tarp or a couple of trash bags because shopping for your garden can be a messy process. Wear the aforementioned hat, sunscreen, and sturdy shoes.

BACK AT THE NURSERY

When plants are on display, their pots are generally packed as tightly together as possible. Because all the blooms and branches are commingled, plants sometimes look more robust than they truly are and appear to have more buds and flowers than they actually do. Survey the display and choose a specimen you think looks good. Separate the pot from its surroundings to get a realistic view of the plant without the support of its peers. If you're purchasing six-packs or flats of six-packs, at least examine the grouping to see that they look healthy.

Some experts say to tap the plant out of its pot and inspect the root system. I've never had the nerve to do this. I check to see if roots are coming out the hole in the bottom of the plant (it's fine if a few little ones are) and to see if it looks sturdy with a good balance of buds and greenery.

If you're gutsier than I am, though, and want to make sure a plant is good enough to go in your garden, hold the bottom of the pot in one hand. With the fingers of your other hand spread across the top of the pot, support the lowest branches. Turn the pot over and gently ease the plant out.

If the roots are all tightly wound around and around inside the pot and there seem to be more of them than soil, the plant is pot bound. While that isn't an ideal situation, you can plant it anyway if you first unwind the roots a bit. You can even take a pair of garden shears or a knife and cut the roots at the bottom to free them so they can grow out from the plant rather than in an ever-tighter spiral.

If you tap out a plant and see no roots at all, and the soil falls away to reveal more of the same, pass up that plant in favor of one that's ready to go home with you. Leave the other in the nursery to grow some more.

Of course, since we're always looking for ways to save time, the well-rooted plant is your best bet.

"INSTALLMENT" SHOPPING

You'll soon get a feel for which plants are healthy and strong, so the process of selecting and buying plants won't take as long as you'd think. What might hold you up, though, is the long line of other gardeners who want to buy their plants at exactly the same time you do.

If you run out of time and can't make all the selections at once, or the ka-ching of the cash register is making you dizzy, that's just fine. Because you want to plant your purchases as soon after getting them home as possible, it's a good idea to break your garden shopping into installments.

You've already amended your soil and it's ready and waiting for the plants. Why not start with the tall bedding annuals and/or perennials? Since you'll be planting them in the back of a border or the middle of an island garden, they'll be the first ones in. You can go back for the others as you're ready for them. Or start with one entire flower bed and save the rest for other trips.

THE GOOD NEWS

This all becomes easier the second year, and easier still in subsequent years. Why?

- Because you're going to keep a record of how many and which annuals you buy, as well as when you plant them.
- Because you're going to sprinkle some perennials into the mix, so that with luck and careful tending, those are plants you won't have to purchase again for the same spot. Instead, you'll greet

them each spring and summer as old friends. You can add to your collection of perennials over the years, selecting new ones that sound interesting and appropriate for your garden.

- Because you'll be able to refer to your planting plan, on which you've mapped out all the plants, so you'll know just where to look for emerging perennials.

- And finally, because you're going to keep track of your successes—and, alas, your failures—and learn from both.

27

planting your purchases

As much as we can't wait to buy out the nursery, once we get the new additions home, we often treat them like Dickensian orphans. We haul them out of the car and dump them unceremoniously in a dark corner by the garage. Other, more pressing matters call for our attention, and these foundlings— er, seedlings—wait and wait, and then wait some more, for our tender ministrations. If we think to provide sustenance (water), the hardy ones hang on; the weak ones perish. Before long, even the fittest of the survivors begin to flag.

What were we thinking? Now that we have these dozens, or hundreds, of needy little things in our possession, how are we going to find time for them? The thought of taking each and every one out of its six-pack or pot or mesh bag and putting it in the right place—and then caring for it! It's overwhelming!

Yes, it is daunting—if you look at it that way. But leaving your plant purchases moldering in their temporary homes is wasteful and yes, even cruel. Besides you've already put in time selecting and buying the plants—and you don't want that time, as well as the money you spent, to go to waste.

What to do? As with most tasks, if you break it up into smaller components, the job gets easier and gets accomplished sooner. Just do it.

You already have your plan (right?) and know where you want the plants to go. Grab a trowel and spend 15 minutes planting while the casserole's baking or while you're waiting for your kids to get home from school. Instead of sleeping in on a Saturday, set the alarm and head for the garden. You'll be surprised how much you'll get done, and you'll feel good about your accomplishments. Besides, the sooner you get the plants in

ABA

you position your new plants that the conditions you observed or guessed at truly exist. Is it sunny where you're going to put your vegetables, or now that the nearby tree has leafed out, is there more shade than sun? Is the ground soggier here than it was when you did your landscape plan? If you find any surprises, now is the time to replan accordingly. Otherwise you'll need to move plants later if they fail to thrive—or, worse yet, you'll lose them.

Using your planting plan, choose what you consider a good spot for the plant or plants. Then, before you dig a single hole, save yourself some time down the road by giving yourself a preview. Set the plants on the ground, in their pots, and then stand back and take a good look. Juggle the pots around until you like the arrangement, keeping in mind that, once they're in the ground, the plants will be lower by about the height of the pot. If a plant is lopsided, now's the time to decide which way it should face to create the most pleasing effect.

Before you begin digging holes, position as many pots as possible where you want them. That way, you'll be able to see how they'll look together and whether you'll need to make another trip to the garden center right away to buy more plants. Experience and planning can save you those extra trips, but at first you might just need to spend a little more time to get the look you want.

the ground, the sooner they'll grow big and strong and beautiful.

If this little motivational speech isn't enough to goad you into action, maybe you can con or convince your friends and family to do the planting. After all, you did the planning and made the purchases; maybe now they'll let you sit back and direct the show.

Just keep in mind that time is of the essence.

LOCATION, LOCATION

That said, where are you going to put your new plants? You've already made your decisions while going through the planning process. Now, make sure as

the spare-time gardener

One way to avoid too many repeat shopping trips is to buy more plants than you think you'll need for this particular garden and then use any extras in other parts of the yard or in containers. That's where having a unified plan comes in handy, since what works in one area of your property will probably work in others.

HEDGE YOUR BETS WITH CONTAINER GARDENING

If you're still in doubt about whether some plants are suitable for particular spots, why not plant them in containers? If selected and planted with care, these make a nearly perfect place to try out annual flowers and vegetables, and sometimes even shrubs without a lot of the hassle that goes with planting them in the ground. And, of course, flowers and foliage plants look just wonderful tumbling out of good-looking containers.

If you need to, you can move the whole arrangement to a sunnier (or shadier) spot. In a container, you can also experiment with color in bolder and more innovative ways than you might in a large border.

Feel free to plant perennials in containers, even in areas where they won't winter over successfully. Watch them thrive on your patio all summer and then, in the fall (the best time to plant perennials), dig a hole and put them in a spot in your garden so you can enjoy them year after year. However, way back in the spring, before you ever buy these perennials for container use, have an idea of where you might want to give them a permanent home come fall.

TIMING IS EVERYTHING

How early in the season can you plant annuals and vegetables? When should you plant perennials? Check with your garden center. The experts there will know the planting dates for your area, which correspond with the last average frost date and vary according to the hardiness of the plants you're using. When's the best time to fertilize? They'll know that, too, since it's tied in with when you plant.

You may be able to fudge a little and plant earlier than recommended, especially in protected, sunny spots in your yard; but don't be surprised if a late frost sends you back to square one. If you're trying to save time, you don't want to have to cover over your plants during a cold snap.

Perennials can be successfully planted anytime between spring and fall. If you plant them in the spring, wait until the ground has heated up a bit and the soil is not heavily compacted with moisture left over from winter. If you plant in summer, beware of the heat, and provide plenty of water. Fall is a good time to plant; but make it early enough so the roots have some time to spread out and become established before the first frost. Your plants will thank you.

PLANTERS' PROCRASTINATION

Timing is also an issue when you first bring home your plants, or receive them through the mail. If you can't plant them right away, there are some ways to keep your purchases happy and healthy until you can. But don't make them wait too long; write yourself a note, tie a string around your finger, or do whatever else it takes to remind you that they need planting. Out of sight, out of mind is not a theory you want to test in the garden.

- If plants are in pots when you buy them, and the weather is warm enough, place them outside, pot and all, in a bright, sheltered spot. If the soil appears to be drying out, and you *still* can't find time to plant them, then give them enough water to keep them alive.
- If you purchase bare-root woody plants with no soil or even leaves, cover the roots with damp newspaper or paper toweling in a plastic bag. These should be kept in a darker spot than the potted plants until you can plant them,

which, to protect your investment, should be soon.
- Perennial roots can be kept in the refrigerator for a few days, stored in the bags in which they arrive.
- When you buy or receive bulbs by mail (always make sure it's the correct planting time), open the bag to promote air circulation. Then store them in a cool, dry location until planting.

GIVING YOUR PLANTS THE RIGHT TIME OF DAY

There are other timing considerations as to the best way to plant, water, and feed your garden.

- What's the best time of day to plant? Some say first thing in the morning; others say late afternoon. I say the best time is when you *have* time.
- The same is true of watering, although it's best not to spray plants' foliage during the heat of the day. It may be a fiction, but rumor has it that the water refracts the light, which in turn can "burn" the leaves. I believe that watering is best done in the early morning, if possible, so the garden can spend the day soaking up the moisture. Nights are often cool, and watering in the evening

could leave plants damp and cool, conditions that could lead to disease.

- If you really get serious about gardening, you might want to install a drip irrigation system to water your flower and vegetable gardens. The cost up front is a little steep, but all you do is turn a knob and your garden is watered. If turning a knob is too much for you, you can put the entire system on a timer. Your extension service can give you all the information you need.

PLANTING POINTERS

Once you have your garden beds dug and cleared of sticks and stones and any plants you don't want there (maybe you'd like to try them somewhere else in your landscape), there are ways to help make your garden a success. Never fear: Plants *want* to grow. If you give them the right conditions and care, they'll express their gratitude with growth and flowers.

Never allow your plants to look like soldiers in a row. Even if you stagger the rows, as you look at the garden from an angle, all you'll see between the straight lines of plants is empty soil. It's just as easy—easier in fact—to plant in a random line as to even up every seedling with a ruler and string. Gardens should be graceful and natural looking. Ideally, they should look as though they spring from the earth in a perfect harmony of line and color with no help from you, the gardener.

You've decided where and how you want to arrange the plants. Place a tarp, flattened trash bag or bucket, or wheelbarrow if necessary, next to the *small, manageable area* where you'll start to plant. Putting the soil from the holes you'll dig directly on the ground is only a good idea if there are no other plants around, and if you can put the soil someplace where you won't need to dig for another new plant.

Starting with a plant you want to place towards the back of the area you're planting, put your fingers around the stem at soil level, turn the pot and plant and all upside down, and gently coax the root ball out of the pot. Gently tapping the pot on the side with a trowel will help recalcitrant plants leave the safety of their containers (if it's a clay pot and it breaks, save the pieces to use as shards in the bottoms of containers).

Using that same trowel, or a shovel if it's a big plant, dig a hole just slightly larger and deeper than the root ball. As you dig. If your soil is dense and clay-like in spite of the compost you've added, poke around in the soil a little deeper and wider than the hole to loosen it a bit.

A gardening friend advises to "dig a five-dollar hole for a fifty-cent plant." Sometimes, however, you'll dig down only to find that there's a root or a big stone in your way. Shift your shovel position little by little and keep digging until the obstruction is no longer a problem. If it's a really big rock (ledge) or the roots are too big and thick to be cut or to allow you to plant among them, you may have to re-think your plan. You could plant something that requires less of a hole—plugs of ground covers, for instance. Or you can always plunk a container garden down on the site without ever digging a hole.

Keep a hose with a "programma-ble" nozzle or watering wand by your side so you can put some water in each hole just before adding the plant. Set the plant in the hole and jiggle it around a little, adding back a bit of the soil you removed so the roots have a firm footing with no space underneath them. Then fill in the spaces at the sides. Don't pile soil up around the stem; the crown of the plant, where it met the soil in its original pot, should be right at the surface. Give each plant a drink as soon as it's planted.

Repeat with all your plants. This takes less time to do than to read about and becomes easier with practice.

After all the plants are in the ground, turn the hose on them with the sprayer set to a gentle shower. Think deep thoughts, admire your handi-work, plan your next party or grocery list or garden, or simply "veg out"; but stay there until you've given every one of your new additions a good stiff drink. They need it.

Now's a good time to add another layer of compost, or fine mulch if you prefer. It will keep in the moisture and nip any weeds in the bud.

CREATE A PATCH OF COLOR—AND THEN ANOTHER

If you have more than one variety of a species that comes in many colors—daylily, for example—they'll look more beautiful if you put three or five or more clumps of one plant in an area and then choose for the adjoining area plants that are the closest to the first plant's color, and so on until you have a smooth gradation from one shade and hue to another.

PLANTING ANNUALS

Annuals provide a lot of bloom for your buck; otherwise, we'd all simply rely on perennials. Sure it's more time consuming to bring in new plants every year to replace the ones that died off the previous year, but if they're in the right spot and receive enough water and fertilizer, annuals can outshine a lot of your tried-and-true perennials. For a bigger show in less time, plant annual seedlings closer together than recommended.

PLANTING PERENNIALS

While there's a lot of wiggle room when it comes to annuals, you plant perennials for the long haul. Since you'll be living with them for years—maybe a lifetime—it makes sense to plant them with a lot of care and consideration.

PLANTING GROUND COVERS

Ground covers often come in forms that make them a little difficult to transplant to your garden. Some arrive in straggly bundles of plants tied together with string, so your chore is to separate the bundles, straggle and all, into individual plants. Others come in flats of 100, with their roots all tangled into a nearly inextricably mesh. Gently pull and pry them apart as you plant them.

Ground covers should be planted where they'll do best, whether in sun or shade, wet or dry. No matter where you place them, water the plants thoroughly after they're in the ground.

PLANTING BULBS

Since the recommended planting depth for bulbs is sometimes as much as six or eight inches, it's easiest to select spots where there are no roots or stones. Planting them in the lawn presents problems: You can't mow the lawn until the flowers have faded, even though by that time in spring it will need cutting; and foliage shouldn't be cut, even after the flowers are gone. Planting bulbs in flower beds is best and easiest, since the soil is clearer and emerging plants will camouflage foliage that remains.

Plant your bulbs en masse, both for the effect it will produce and because it makes the job of planting much easier. If you want to dig out a lot of soil down to the proper planting depth, and then place the bulbs and gently cover over the whole area at one time, go for it. That's a viable alternative if your soil is without stones or has perfect texture.

The rest of us can learn from the pros. Their time is money, so they find the most time-effective methods. Take a giant-economy-sized bag of bulbs and a good sturdy trowel. Kneel down (knee pads or a kneeler is a good idea) and plunge the trowel into the ground deep enough that the hole will be just slightly more than the suggested planting depth. Push it away from you so it leaves enough room for the bulb, and drop in the bulb, root side down (this is usually the flatter side). Cover up the bulb, and lightly tamp down the soil over it. Then, without changing your kneeling place, plant as many bulbs as you can, all spaced within six or eight inches of each other. If you run out of reach before you run out of bulbs, shift your kneeling pad a few feet and continue the process.

Some people like to sprinkle bonemeal in the hole while planting bulbs; they then add a sprinkling on top of the soil as well. Bonemeal can attract skunks and other critters that will happily munch away on your bulbs and leave you nothing to show for your hard work but a tidy hole in the ground for each one they ate. Save your time and money.

There are bulbs that must be planted in the fall, and others that go in the ground in the spring. Usually, the ones you see for sale are available at the correct planting times, but it doesn't hurt to check.

part four

Keep Growing
in Your Spare Time

28

growing the plants

Keeping your garden healthy isn't as hard as you may think, or as hard as others make it appear. The plant kingdom has done quite well without us for a very long time, thank you; and if you've chosen and planted wisely, you can spend only as much time as you can spare and still have a garden that will make you happy.

One caveat: As soon as you get even some or all of your plants in the ground, don't think you can just sit back and take in the show. You have to start caring for them from day one. Neglecting your garden can backfire, since it's a whole lot easier to tend it well in the first place than to get rid of weeds that have become too comfortable in their surroundings or, worse still, pull out dead plants you've purchased, buy new ones, and replant.

GOLD FOR THE GARDEN

Adding compost (organic matter) is one of the very best things you can do for your garden. This magical element, often referred to as "black gold," enriches the soil and improves the texture. It's especially important for gardens where the soil hasn't been amended in the past or where it's been overtaxed.

Compost can be the end result of aging and "cooking" all kinds of natural ingredients, some of which sound pretty unsavory. In the compost-making process, however, these products are transformed into an extremely beneficial substance (offal isn't so awful after all). The label should tell its origins, so check it out if you're squeamish and want to know what you're adding to your garden. No matter what the source, by the time you buy compost in bags, it should be odorless and show no signs of its past existence.

Spread two or three inches of compost over your garden beds, as if it were mulch. Because it *is* mulch. It keeps water in and weeds out, as mulch does. It's easier to extract weeds from a garden covered with a porous layer of compost. Besides, it looks better than most mulches, and unlike some mulch, it doesn't leach nutrients from the soil.

If you're looking for a new and exciting hobby, you might want to make your own compost from leaves, grass clippings, and kitchen scraps (do not use meat, pet poop, or really sturdy vegetables, though). Garden centers carry ready-made compost bins that can get you started and make the job easier. Then, if you find that you like churning out gorgeous, valuable gold for your garden, you may decide to become a more serious composter. Your garden center will be happy to oblige with all the accoutrements of this popular pastime.

KEEPING THEM GREEN AND BLOOMING

Fertilizer does wonders. The right kind and the right amount at the right time, that is. Otherwise, you're just wasting *your* time and can even do harm; you'll have leggier greenery and too much of it, or what should be green will be yellow, or flowers will be minimal.

This is where your soil test comes in handy. The recommendations you'll receive will tell you how much to fertilize plants in different areas of your garden, and it will tell you what formulations to use for what you want to grow. Follow these guidelines, and you'll be in clover.

Here's some good news for spare-time gardeners: You can stop fertilizing perennials in August. If you promote new growth this late in the season, the plants may not make it through the winter. You can continue feeding annuals, though, although the law of diminishing returns comes into play in late summer.

WHEN TO WATER

While it's a good idea for all of us to save water in whatever ways we can, you have a major investment of time and money in your garden and you don't want to lose plants because they don't get enough moisture. You can water effectively and not waste water or time in the process. Remember, too, that an excess of water is as bad as not enough.

One way to save time and help your plants grow strong is to water thoroughly—but only when your garden needs it. Then let the soil get almost dry before you take the time to water it again. If a rainstorm is in the forecast, why not let nature do your watering for you? Use a rain gauge to determine

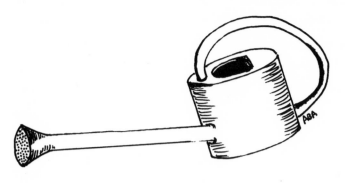

how much precipitation has fallen in any given time period. A half-inch of rain per week might be enough to keep you from having to water your garden. Of course, it depends on the amount of heat and sun, the kinds of plants you grow, and other factors.

Wherever possible, water the soil and roots rather than the foliage and flowers. Unfortunately, automatic sprinklers and watering cans you have to fill and refill don't do the best job. If you have a hand sprayer or a water wand on your hose, try to direct a gentle stream at the plants' roots and be patient enough to soak the soil (you're not going for soggy, though). If you can install a drip irrigation system or a soaker hose, you'll save time and water, and your plants will be healthier.

Morning is a good time to water your plants. Late afternoon will work too, but midday when the sun's beating down is not the best time for you to be watering. You might not have much choice if you have to be at work or other aspects of your life intrude into your gardening. While going out during the noonday sun

may only be for mad dogs and Englishmen, water when you can—and let nature do the job whenever possible. You'll hear from your plants if they're not getting enough to drink.

Deadheading both annuals and perennials can do wonders for your garden, and it's something you can do in your spare time. Take a turn around the garden with a coffee cup in one hand and a basket or bucket in the other. Pick off flowers that have gone by and toss them in the receptacle at hand. You don't have to get to every one every time, but if you do a little deadheading on a regular basis, you can make a real difference in your garden's appearance. In many plants, you'll also prolong the blooming season.

Some plants are so densely covered in flowers that deadheading would take far more time than you want to spend—unless you're looking for a mindless activity that'll keep you out in the fresh air and sunshine. If you'd rather take a shortcut, though, take shears to these plants instead. Just cut off the tops of the stems where most of the flowers are, but don't attack all the stems at once. If you have just one or two plants in one location, give each one a "spotty" haircut, cutting a swath here and there to remove about a third of the stem ends. Yes, this will remove some good flowers along with the decrepit; but you'll end up with a better, longer-lasting display with less work. If you have several of a specific plant, give them their haircuts one at a time so you'll stagger the blooms.

WHAT IS A WEED—REALLY?

One gardener's weed is another gardener's wildflower—or salad. After all, if it's green, it's green. So embrace your weeds, at least some of them, because trying to keep all of them at bay can take much too much of your time.

On the other hand, there are weeds that really detract from the way a garden looks; and these should be dispatched with complete sangfroid. Show no mercy when you have a neat little flower garden and a big, fat weed shoots up in the middle of it overnight. Weeds don't look good in container gardens either, and in vegetable plots they can take vital nutrients from your hard-won soil.

Once you get to know where all your plants are and what they look like as they emerge, you can cull the weeds from among what you want to keep. You'll get to recognize different types of weeds even when they're tiny shoots, and that's the best time to get rid of them without disturbing your plantings.

STAKING AND CAGING

These may sound like something nasty right out of the Dark Ages, but they're really ways to be kind to your plants. Wind and heavy rain can make even the tallest, straightest ornamentals flop over into an unsightly heap. Unless a tall plant has a very sturdy stem and gets plenty of sun to keep it strong, it's important to help it keep its good posture. For a plant with a single stem, a stake works fine. If it has multiple stems, a cage helps the plant keeps its shape without compressing it. Unless you're using them as ground covers, vining and twining plants need something to grow on. Stakes and cages can provide the support they need, too.

Natural materials (bamboo or wood) are good choices, and black or dark-green metal stakes or cages can be strong yet unobtrusive. Some plants come with supports when you buy them; you can either use these or, if you don't like their looks, replace them with your own.

If using stakes, insert them close to the stem carefully when you put new plants in the ground, or when returning plants are up to about a quarter to a third of their full height. The length should be a few inches shorter than the plant will be at its tallest. Secure each plant to its stake loosely and gently using paper-and-metal ties or strips of cloth. Old pantyhose make great plant ties because of their stretchy fabric.

Cages, which are usually a horizontal grid supported on several sticks or stakes, should be inserted around an emerging plant when it's less than the height of the grid made to support the mature growth. Then, every few days, make sure to gently fold any wayward stems through the holes. It's okay if a few stems are on the outside of the grid. You can make your own cage by inserting several sticks or stakes into the ground and weaving string among them to create a support for your plants.

HEALTH CARE BENEFITS FOR PLANTS

A little time-saving advice: Don't bother trying to redeem plants that are just hanging on by a thread. Sure, you'd have the satisfaction of saving a living thing, but the longer I garden, the more I realize it just isn't worth the time and effort. And you're hearing this from someone who has a hard time even cutting flowers to bring inside because they look so happy and alive in the garden.

If a plant looks vaguely dissatisfied, you might try moving it to another spot (my neighbors have a "rehab center" in an out-of-the-way part of their garden). However, if a plant is scraggly and sickly to the point where relocating it or applying a little judicious pruning isn't going to help, pull it out and start over. Some nurseries or catalogues offer guarantees. If a plant doesn't survive and you have the time, call them and ask for a replacement or refund.

In any case, replace it with a thriving specimen, and it will brighten your garden and your outlook.

GARDEN WITH ECOLOGY IN MIND

So much of what we do in the garden affects the environment that it pays to be mindful of the products and practices we use.

To save both resources and time, and even some money, I practically never water my lawn. Sure, it gets a little tawny come late summer, but it always spruces up again after a good rain. If it truly gets so dry that I think it will perish, I give it a good soaking once a week until weather conditions "improve"; that is, improve from the lawn's point of view. It's so sad to see sprinklers going full blast just after, or even during, a good rainy day. And it's worse still when they're inadvertently set to spray sidewalks and driveways. What a waste!

Fertilizers can be expensive, so make sure you abide by the recommendations you receive with your soil test results. Then, when you purchase the correct product, apply it according to the package directions. Why waste your money and time applying the wrong fertilizer in the wrong amount at the wrong time when it's so easy to do it right?

As with weeds, it helps to develop a little tolerance for pests. If something's chomping away at your foliage, try the least invasive methods. Before bringing on the bug sprays, you can handpick Japanese beetles and slugs or capture earwigs in damp, rolled-up newspaper.

It's always a good idea to know what you're killing, too. Some insects look menacing but are beneficial and should be left to forage on the true culprits. By investing in a little bug book and identifying the insects in your garden, you might save time, money, *and* the environment.

CONTAINERS—A DIFFERENT BALLGAME

With only a few steps and regular maintenance, containers alone or in groups can have a major impact on your landscape. They're easy to plant and tend, but, as you may recall from our earlier foray into container gardening, there are a few points to remember:

- Make sure you have drainage holes in the bottom of the container, and cover them with shards, coffee filters, or newspaper before adding the soil.
- Use good potting mix, not soil from your garden. You can make it yourself by sterilizing regular soil or, easier by far, purchase it in big bags. If you use untreated soil from the garden, you run the

risk of adding weed seeds, diseases, pests, and other problems to the relatively small, enclosed environment of a container. And who needs that?

- Add an all-purpose or slow-release fertilizer to the soil in the container before you insert the plants. This step will help the foliage and blooms flourish and will also save you the time of having to sprinkle the fertilizer between the stems and work it in once your container is tightly planted.
- Depending on what you plant, they may need a lot of sun, as much as six to eight hours a day.

Containers have so many good points that it's sometimes easy to forget their one drawback: They need lots of watering and fertilizing. When displayed at ground level, they also sometimes provide what your cat might see as an attractive outdoor litter box or simply a place to play in the dirt. To keep Kitty out of the container, spread pebbles over the top; this is the easy way. Or, if you're only putting one plant in a pot—a tomato, say—and don't mind a little more work, you can cut a circle of wide-mesh screening and cut another hole in the middle to accommodate the size the stem will be when the plant is mature. Then cut a slit from the edge to the center, and fit it around the stem. Pebbles work fine, though.

Feel free to move containers around your garden, although once large pots are planted you might need a hand truck or be tempted to hire a crane. That's where careful planning pays off: Plant the pot where you want it to spend the summer.

29

keeping the plants in check

It may seem counterintuitive, but once your garden is established and your plants are thriving, it's time to take them down a peg or two. There are several reasons for cutting into your plants:

- You can extend the bloom of flowering plants by "deadheading" them.
- You should keep shrubs and trees in scale with the rest of your plantings through judicious pruning.
- You want to keep your plants healthy and allow air to circulate so you don't have to deal with powdery mildew or other problems.
- You might want to train a plant into a particular shape.
- You can make new plants by cutting apart and dividing those that

spread, and the original specimens will benefit in the process.

WHEN THE BLOOM IS OFF THE ROSE— OR ANYTHING ELSE

For some flowering plants, you can increase the bloom time and the number of blossoms by cutting or pinching off spent flowers. These has-beens allow the plant to think it's done its job of reproduction and can now relax in the sun for the rest of the summer. You have to interrupt its idyll and let it know there's still work to be done.

To do this, remove both the flowers that have wilted and the seed pods that develop at their base. This is more effective in producing additional bloom in some plants than in others. Try it on marigolds, pansies, zinnias, calendulas, cosmos, and petunias.

In these and other plants, whether deadheading produces extra blooms or not, it makes the plants look neater. Picture a bright-red annual geranium full of brilliant flowers. Now picture the same plant with the dried, brownish remains of flowers interspersed throughout the colorful blooms. It ruins the effect, and yet just a minute spent snapping off the offending stems can help the plant look its best and keep it healthier too.

PRUNING POINTERS

Before you buy shrubs and trees, ask about the recommended pruning time and techniques. With most spring-blooming shrubs, for example, you should wait until they've finished blooming before you give them a haircut. Otherwise, you'll cut off this year's blooms. Some hydrangeas can be cut clear back to the ground in early spring every few years and still return healthy and happy to bloom that same season. With overgrown lilacs and forsythias, if you take out a third of the branches

each year, after three years you'll have a rejuvenated plant. You can repeat the procedure as needed.

If you want to do some pruning yourself, rather than letting a pro handle the job, please don't go for the lollipop effect—little round balls of shrubbery dotted about the landscape. It's time consuming and, frankly, kind of weird looking. To save time, and create a more pleasing effect, let the natural habit or shape of a shrub be your guide. Forsythia looks lovely in a graceful fountain shape. A lilac should be allowed to reach for the sky, within reason. Unless you're to the manor born—and still live in the manor—the 20-foot-high hedge is more trouble than it's worth. Just think of the ladder you'll need!

If you have large shrubs and trees that have gotten out of hand, it might be time to call in the experts. A tree service may cost a bit, or a lot, depending on how far gone your plants and trees are; but for the sake of safety, saving your precious time, and getting it right, it might be worth it. You can start with a free estimate and then have all or part of the job done. At least you'll know where you stand and won't be using guesswork.

Whether you do all or some of the work yourself, play it safe. Wear goggles and sturdy gloves and shoes. Don't try to do too much of the job at one time, and don't try to cut off too large a portion of a plant at any one time either.

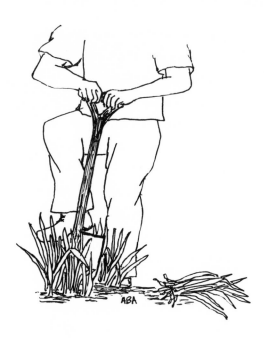

DIVIDE AND CONQUER

It's a real treat—and takes less time than a trip to the garden center—to divide perennials and create new (free!) plants for your garden or to share.

Many perennials take well to being divided in early spring. It eliminates cramped plants and gives them a chance to grow up to their potential; and for very little work you get new additions at no cost.

Hosta and daylily divisions are particularly successful. The best time to divide these hefty perennials is when they're first beginning to emerge. Decide, based on the size of the plant and how long it's been since it was di-

vided, how many new plants you want to generate. There are several methods; here are a couple of them.

For the first, you'll need two long-handled garden forks. Insert them, with their tines back to back, into the middle of the clump, avoiding stems as far as possible. Gently pry the plant and roots apart by using the handles as leverage. That's the kinder method, but it takes equipment you might not have and is a little more time consuming.

Another way is to take a sharp spade, line it up so it's between stems, and then step on it hard to shove it down through the roots. Some of the roots will be cut, but the plant will still survive and continue to spread.

Dig out the part you want to move to a new spot, and fill in around the part of the plant you're leaving in place. If you want to create more than one new plant, repeat the process with the clump you've dug up. Then plant your new divisions in a spot where they'll have the right conditions to thrive.

If you do this correctly, and don't get greedy and take off so much that you send the parent plant into the slough of despair, you'll never notice the difference in the old plant; and the new ones will make a nice, free addition to your garden.

30
weed this and reap

Weeds! Just the word is enough to give you the shivers. You think of rundown yards around ramshackle houses. You imagine coarse, prickly leaves and interminable, stubborn roots. Nothing

can keep them down, except maybe our garden blowtorch.

The thing is that if you took a closer look at the rundown yard around the ramshackle house, you'd see that many of the plants are green and flourishing, and some may even be wildflowers.

You probably want a yard that's neater and cleaner looking, but it may be time to rethink the concept of "weed." Gardeners often have this concept that if they haven't planted it themselves, or didn't mean it to be there, and it's in *their* garden, it's evil.

Relax. Repeat this mantra: If it's green, it's good. . . . If it's green, it's good.

A WEED BY ANY OTHER NAME

What is a weed anyway? It's whatever you don't like and don't want in your garden. It's an invasive plant that chokes out its neighbors.

One man's weed is another man's posy. If you like the looks of something, and it doesn't appear to be taking over and intimidating your other plants, keep it in.

Dandelions—the focus of many diabolical instruments of weed torture—are cheerful little things. Make salad. Make wine. Make soup. Seriously, the first green shoots of dandelions make terrific salad greens. You might even be buying them in those pricey bags of "baby greens" at the supermarket or farm stand. Beware of eating them, however, if you've used pesticides or herbicides on your lawn.

Before you start weeding furiously, look around and decide which plants really bother you and which you can live with. This is partly a function of location. A weed you may want to pull from your dooryard garden could be left alone out in the far reaches of the backyard.

There are some weeds you should tackle without mercy before they spread:

- Those that were uninvited but will nonetheless invade your lawn and garden and become increasingly hard to eradicate (e.g., quack grass)
- Vines that will strangle out other plants

- Plants whose seeds will spread and create havoc (e.g., thistle)
- Those that can harm you and yours (e.g., poison ivy, brambles)
- Perennials you purchased as ornamentals that become invasive (e.g., the dreaded aegopodium)

Then there are other weeds with which you might want to be more lenient, either because they're pretty or because they're useful:

- Plants with flowers and foliage you like (incredible as it may seem, these "weeds" could include wildflowers of many types, including violets, Jack-in-the-pulpit, Solomon's-seal, and on and on)
- Volunteers of plants you've grown in the past that reseed themselves in unexpected places (many species)
- Plants that provide color or salad greens. Just try not to let them go to seed. But if they do, carefully remove and dispose of the seed heads as soon as they appear or, better yet, before they spring open only to spread by the thousands all over your yard. Please don't put them in the compost pile, or they'll think of it as their own private nursery.

the spare-time gardener

CHOKE 'EM OUT

The best way to attack weeds is never to let them get a purchase in the first place. Be proactive. Plant your ornamentals so densely that the weeds can't get through. Use ground covers extensively. Mulch so deeply with compost and/or shredded bark or hulls that the weeds can't find their way to the sun. Two or more inches of compost should do it. Any weeds that do manage to grow will have a tenuous foothold because of the porosity of the mulch, and you'll be able to pull them out easily—much to everyone's but the weed's satisfaction.

Some gardeners like to lay down black (or red!) plastic, or what's called landscape cloth, and then cut holes through which their annuals can grow. The plastic can keep weeds from growing by starving them of sunlight. In vegetable gardens, strips of plastic between the rows can also be used. Working plastic or landscape cloth around established perennials is more difficult, unless the plants are in strictly regimented rows and strips of plastic or cloth can be spread between the rows.

Watering a garden covered in plastic can be a little tricky, and the overall effect can be artificial. Weighing down the edges or corners is a good idea. If you decide to try plastic or cloth, I'd suggest starting with a small area and then expanding it the next year if you find it works for you. If looks are an issue, you can camouflage the plastic by spreading a layer of mulch over it.

HOW TO WEED

You're bound to have some weeds. Most nasty weeds produce flowers and seeds. The best practice is to pull or dig these out before they have a chance to produce either. Dispose of your weeds wisely. If you want to compost them, try not to add the seeds; and then make sure the compost "cooks" to a temperature that will kill any roots and remaining seeds that could make new plants.

To get rid of weeds, you'll probably want to use tools for some and pull out others by hand—a very satisfying way of getting rid of your aggressions. If you have a large area that's covered in weeds and nothing else, and you have plenty of time before you want that garden area to look good, you can cover the ground with plastic sheeting and wait until the weeds cook. Then they'll give up without a fight.

It's easiest to do your hand weeding when the ground is wet, or even while it's raining (good for the complexion too). When the soil is "slippery," even the most tenacious weeds are easier to pull, and some will slide right out for you. If there are thorns involved, be sure to wear sturdy gloves.

Procrastinators beware: It's easiest to get rid of weeds when they're young. When they're smaller, they haven't put down deep roots. If you start early, before they get a foothold, you won't give them a chance to deplete the soil of nutrients, steal water from the plants you *want* to grow, or choke out good plants to make room for their weedy compatriots. However, you run the risk of pulling out perfectly good plants, thinking they're weeds sprouting. That's an argument for following your planting plan and then mapping your gardens in your garden notebook so you'll know what's planted where. It's also a reason for getting to know what plants look like as they emerge.

While weeds' ever-sturdier roots are cause for early action, another reason to get to your weeds early is so they won't set seeds that can spread and spread . . . and spread. Dandelions alone can produce more than 10,000 of those fuzzy little parachutes we all puffed on when we were kids so we could watch them scatter hither and yon. No wonder there are so many dandelions in the world today!

For eons it seems, inventors have been trying to build a better weedtrap so the world will beat a path to their doors by way of their weed-free yard. Some of these devices work, and some don't. Some are as simple as a scuffle hoe you pull across a row, and others require engineering degrees to operate.

Different tools will appeal to different gardeners. Browse the garden tool section to see which tools seem to be likely prospects. Beware of gizmos that are complicated to operate, require batteries, have hot or sharp parts that could be dangerous to you as well as to your weeds, or use nasty chemicals.

That brings us to the controversial subject of herbicides. I don't like them; but then again, I only have a quarter-acre of yard to tend.

My husband has bought me some mean-looking weeding machines, and one day I'll work up my courage to try them all. Till then, I'll attack weeds in my yard with an uncomplicated array of tools: a spade for big areas, a smaller trowel or digging implement for smaller patches, and my hands for individual weeds or tightly planted areas.

There are exceptions to every rule. The blowtorch on a stick is indispensable for removing grass and weeds between walkway and patio stones—far better even than the crooked knives sold for that purpose. Again, if columbine or ferns volunteer, I let them be. I'd advise you to decide what your own personal tolerance level is, and weed accordingly.

the spare-time gardener

31

summing up the season

At the end of the growing season, take a deep breath, sit down, and decide how successful your garden was. Better yet, several times during the season, before this final reckoning, take your garden notebook outside and walk around your yard, making note of what's thriving and what's struggling.

Paying attention to the overall picture, as well as the individual plants and plantings, ask yourself the following questions.

About the Garden as a Whole

1. Do I like the way my garden looks—right now?
2. Which spots are the most appealing?
3. Which spots are weak links in the plan?

4. Am I using the space to its fullest?
5. If not, how else would I like to use it? How can I accomplish that? How much time will it take to accomplish?

About the Plants

1. Is this a plant I'd like to grow again? Should I try a different color? Different size?
2. Do I want these plants to be in the same place, or would they look better and grow better somewhere else?
3. Would more of one or two plants make a better display, or should I try for more variety?
4. What plant discoveries have I made recently?

About Techniques and Tools

1. What growing techniques did I try that worked? Or didn't work?

2. Which tools worked best for my gardening style?

Never fear if a plant—or a whole garden—looks pitiful. Remember, a lot of gardening is like a haircut—if it's cut back, it grows back. If you've managed to kill something with kindness or pull it out inadvertently thinking it's a weed (bye, bye clematis), you can try again next year.

32

the good gardener
vs. the bad seed

Do you sometimes feel that everyone around you knows more about gardening than you do? Do your friends and neighbors toss Latin plant names into general conversation? Is their confidence in their own plantsmanship daunting? After hearing their garden must-do's and have-to's, do you just want to wither on the vine?

First, understand that a lot of their plantsmanship is really one-upmanship. There's a lot about gardening that brings out the best in us; but there's something that also brings out the worst in some .otherwise terrific people. There appears, seemingly out of the blue, a sense of extreme competitiveness about gardening, flower arranging, the perfection of the lawn, or what have you that cuts across age, sex, economic level, or any other

defining characteristic. Was it something in their childhoods? Are they unhappy? Bored? Possibly, but the way this competitiveness manifests itself can be pretty unpleasant or, at best, ridiculous.

Do not become one of these people. As our mothers told us all, be yourself. I've been fortunate to know and work with some titans of landscape architecture and horticulture, as well as of the entertainment world. In both spheres, it's become quite clear that those who are the most gifted are the same ones who don't need to vaunt themselves through posturing or pettiness. Oh sure, sometimes they're flamboyant (that's what makes them fun), but they're confident enough in their own talents that they have no need or desire to belittle anyone else's.

As you hone your gardening skills, revel in your knowledge and abilities; but be generous of spirit. When asked, give advice, but skip the harangue. Lend a hand, but try not to criticize.

Share the bounty of your garden, but accept lesser offerings from others with grace. And always expect other gardeners to return the courtesy.

Herein endeth the sermon.

33

pop quiz—a peek into your garden shed

This is a quiz with only one question:

When I look at my garage, garden shed, or wherever it is I store my gardening tools and supplies, I see (choose one):

(a) An efficiency expert's dream come true

(b) A challenge, but I love challenges—up to a point

(c) The Black Hole of Calcutta

(d) Are you kidding? What garage? What shed? I can't find it!

If you selected (a): How do you do it? Maybe you draw little outlines on the wall to indicate where each tool and implement goes. Maybe you don't have many tools, or conversely, you have a REALLY BIG garage or tool shed. Or you're naturally neat and tidy. Or, most probably, you've made it a point to become organized. And if that's true, more power to you!

What can the rest of us learn from you? Being organized and knowing where everything is saves bundles of time and is, contrary to popular belief, truly possible. If we make the effort to get our storage in order, we'll find the right tool at the right time and we'll know where we put (rather than where we left) the potting soil, and the pots to put it in. It's worth it, if only for the simple peace of mind an orderly space brings. And think of all the time you save.

If you selected (b): We know how you feel. You can find the right tool at the right time—but only some of the time. You're frustrated and know you can do better. Should you have fewer gardening tools and materials, or should you devise a better system for storing them? Make it easy on yourself.

What can the rest of us learn from you? Even with the best of intentions, our garden implements and supplies can get away from us. They end up in a heap in a corner of the garage or sharing shelf space with old boots and batteries. Why not make the extra effort to move as far from (b) to (a) as time and space will allow? You're almost there.

If you selected (c): Most of us have been in your shoes at one time or another. Your life—and the orderly arrangement of objects in it—seems beyond your control. Fortunately, there are solutions and, to use a platitude, there's nowhere to go but up.

What can we learn from you—and vice versa? Every time you rummage through the detritus of your everyday life for tools and other buried treasure, you realize anew that it takes a lot more time than it would if your living and work spaces were more orderly. When things get out of hand, we tell ourselves that even though our garage, office, or what have you looks messy, we know just where everything is under the rubble. Down deep, though, we realize we're just kidding ourselves: Even if we know where something is, we still have to dig into the pile of other stuff to reach it.

If you selected (d): Probably you're just starting out in an apartment or condo, or you've downsized. A lack of storage space takes some getting used to. Maybe you think that you couldn't possibly follow the old adage, "a place

for everything and everything in its place."

What can we learn from you—and you from us? There are two ways to avoid the pending or present chaos. You can devise ingenious ways to store and organize "stuff," or you can jettison old tools you never use and/or avoid bringing items into the house if they aren't necessary and useful.

GET ORGANIZED TO SAVE TIME

Garden tools and supplies are particularly prone to messiness. After all, even though garden gurus forbid us to say so, soil looks and acts like *dirt*, right? And all those handles and jutting metallic objects can get just plain messy.

Keep in mind that even a little investment in organization will save more time than it takes to accomplish. De-cluttering your garden equipment will go a long way to de-clutter your mind and your life. You'll feel better about yourself and your surroundings, too; and before you know it, you'll be de-cluttering your closets and basement.

You don't want your efforts to backfire, however. Rather than deciding in a fit of organizational zeal that you'll clean the entire garage in one day, break the job into manageable chunks. Set an alarm and spend one hour each Saturday, say, organizing. Sometimes, at the end of the hour, you'll be on a

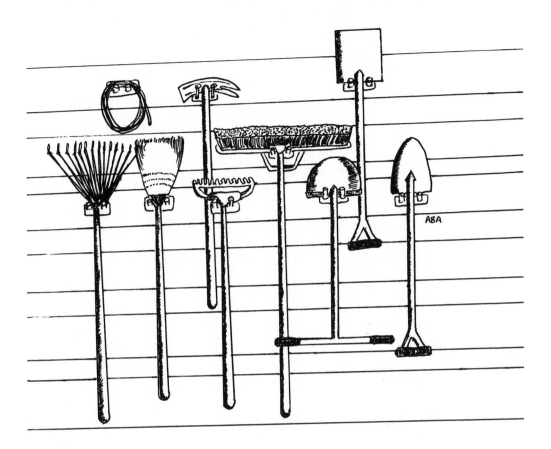

roll and want to keep going. Resist the urge. Sure, take a few more minutes to finish up one area, but remember that if you do something to the point of exhaustion or frustration, you'll never want to go back to the task.

"A place for everything and everything in its place" is nowhere truer than in the realm of garden equipment. Leave a tool in the garden, and it will turn up next spring, bedraggled from a winter out in the elements. Put it away by throwing it in a heap with all the other tools, and you'll have to unravel a Gordian knot of wood and metal to retrieve it. But clean it off and hang it from the same hook each time you're finished using it, and you'll always know where to find it.

Try to keep all your garden implements in one storage area. That way, even if you haven't put something away neatly, you'll have a general idea where it might be. If any are broken, either toss them or fix them. If they're dull, sharpen them or install replacement blades. If you're really energetic and have some time on your hands, you can paint those outlines on the garage wall to show you where specific tools should be hung—and then make sure you hang them there.

34

tools you can, and can't, count on—an opinionated gardener's list

You've heard the expression, "the right tool for the job"? Nowhere is it more essential than in gardening. Tools need to work, of course; but more than that, they need to be comfortable to use and fit in with your gardening style. To accomplish the same task, one person might use a half-dozen tools to another's one or two. Whenever possible use tools that do double duty.

USING THE TOOLS

- Be careful. Gardening can be hazardous to your health. Garden tools can be sharp or hot. They can trip you up and weigh you down. When you're wielding tools is no time to save time. Be careful and methodical, and you will end up being more productive—which, of course, does save time in the long run.

- After you've bought the right tool for the job, use it for the job for which it was meant. If you use your carving knife to weed between the stones on your patio, for example, you'll do damage to the knife and perhaps to yourself. There's always room for improvisation, but be practical and sensible about it.

- To make your in-garden experience pleasant and expeditious, assemble the tools you'll use the most and then keep them handy. In fact, to save time, keep duplicates of your most-used tools— two trowels, two hand pruners, two boxes of trash bags, or whatever you usually have to search for every time you start gardening. Keep one set in the garage or tool shed and another at the opposite end of your house. This will save you endless frustrating hikes.

NOT THE MOST TOOLS— THE *RIGHT* TOOLS

You probably have your own favorite tools. Here's a not-very-long list of the basics that everyone needs.

- *Comfy trowel.* I received as a Christmas present last year the most beautiful trowel I'd ever seen. It was English Racing Green with a cushy padded handle, and it looked as if it could handle anything my garden could dish out. The *very first time* I tried to use that trowel, the bowl and handle parted ways. Now, this was *not* an inexpensive tool, and it sure looked great; but for all practical purposes it was purely decorative. Garden tools are not meant to be pretty (although it's a nice bonus); they're meant to work—hard. Make sure you purchase the sturdiest tools you can find and afford. If they fail you, as this trowel did, take them back, as I did!

- *Spade and/or shovel.* You'll need long-handled digging tools for all kinds of jobs in the garden. I like a rectangular, flat shovel because I can use it as an edging tool. I also dig holes for larger plants with it. A curved spade might be more to your liking.

- *Leaf rake.* With its flexible prongs of bamboo or metal, this is the classic tool for corralling leaves and grass clippings. This old favorite can also be used to gently rake the top of the garden and break up small clods of earth.

- *Cultivating rake.* This sturdy rake consists of fixed prongs attached to a solid bar. It's helpful for smoothing the surface after you've turned over the soil. You can use it as a hoe, too; and tapped gently or not so gently on the soil, as necessary, it can be a clod buster. If you were so inclined, this is the implement you'd use to create the parallel lines and swirls in the sandy or pebbled surface of a Zen meditation garden.

- *Hand pruners.* This is no place to skimp. Again, buy the best you can afford, and they'll last you a lifetime. Bypass blades, which neatly cut stems, are preferable to anvil blades that instead crush them where they're cut. You might have to replace pruner blades someday, but these and other parts are readily available for good pruning shears. You can find pruners at just about any garden center or home center. A little time invested in sharpening pruners that are getting dull will pay off in the long run. Just gently and briefly run a small metal file over the cutting portion of the blade. On the back side of the blade, use a little alcohol to remove dried sap and other gunk. Ergonomics has come to gardening tools; for the utmost in comfort, buy pruners that have a swiveling handle (you'll know them when you see them).

- *Hedge shears and/or loppers.* These can be fancy or not, depending on how much you want to pay. While hand pruners are great for most cutting jobs, shears are good for trimming a lot of deadheads at once. Loppers, especially those with a ratcheting head, make trimming branches much easier.

- *Good hose.* It can be curly, collapsible, or traditional, but it should be sturdy and long enough to get water where you want it. Make sure the nozzle fits securely over the faucet, and add a hose washer if necessary, or you'll waste both water and time. Since washers tend to deteriorate over time, consider replacing them annually. If you use a traditional or collapsible hose, you might want to invest in a few hose guides with swivel tops. These specially designed stakes go into the ground along the edges of flower beds

and protect plants from the hose as you drag it around the yard. You could improvise with sticks or tubes or whatever you can conjure up in your fertile imagination. A hose holder or reel is a useful item, too. It keeps your hose neatly rolled up so you don't have to deal with kinks or trip over it, and your grass won't have yellow lines where you've left the hose to snake around the lawn.

- *Sprayer or wand.* The old thumb-over-the-hose-end routine is counterproductive. A pistol-grip sprayer that allows you a complete range of watering options with the turn of its nozzle, from soft shower to powerful spray, is truly useful. The nozzles that offer several settings never seem to have just the right spray. Long watering wands are the choice of many professionals.

- *Watering can.* There are some times that a hose won't do the trick. Watering cans come in all colors, shapes, sizes, and styles. Some have removable nozzles so you can alternate between a gentle shower and a stream of water. When making your selection, think ease of use. Pick a watering can with a big enough hole at the top that you can fill it easily. One with markings to indicate how much water it contains is helpful, especially if you want to mix fertilizer with the water either for houseplants or your garden and need to know how much to add. Make sure it's big enough for your needs but not so hefty that you can't easily carry it when it's full. Watering cans can be very decorative, but if you buy one and its delicately curving spout spurts water halfway across the room, or drips unrelentingly, take it back to the nursery. Looks aren't everything.

ON YOUR PERSON: SOME PRODUCTS AND TOOLS TO MAKE LIFE SAFER AND SANER

There are some supplies you should not only have on hand, but should also be sure to *use*—for your comfort and for safety's sake.

- *Sunscreen.* Who needs the pain and peril of a sunburn? A bad one can keep you off your feet, and out of the garden, for days. And, while they feel and look wonderful, even tans have gone out of

fashion, and for good reason. About 20 minutes before you head outside, slather on a goodly portion of sunscreen with an SPF of 15 or higher. Don't be stingy with the stuff, and reapply as directed on the package. Many people don't realize that sunscreens have expiration dates. Don't take any chances; check the bottle or box for a date, and jettison the old stuff. Since some stores undoubtedly sell last year's lotions this year, before you buy a bottle or tube, determine how much longer it will last before it's no longer effective.

- *Wide-brimmed hat.* This is your second line of defense against the sun. Whether you choose it in canvas or straw, make sure the weave is dense. Ventilation holes are a good idea, and in a stiff breeze you'll be grateful for a thin chinstrap (you can tuck it up under the hat when the wind isn't blowing). You may have your baseball cap broken in so it fits you like the proverbial glove (a baseball glove?), but wearing it when you garden is a big mistake. Even the long-billed models only protect a portion of your face, neck, and shoulders; and your ears don't stand a chance.
- *Repellent.* Keeping mosquitoes, blackflies, no-see-ums, and other biting insects at bay can be a full-time job—swatting, spraying or slathering; dressing in clothing treated with repellents; or wearing netting over your face or your entire body. Everyone's got favorite repellents. Some people tie fabric softener sheets onto their belt loops or rub torn and crushed basil leaves on the skin to keep mosquitoes away; others are convinced that a particular bath oil sends blackflies packing. You probably have your own "folk repellent." Use it, and if it doesn't work for you, try something else. There are dozens of products available that promise to keep insects away or quell the itching and other symptoms should you be bitten. Some of the repellents are combined with sunscreen. The more powerful formulations (those with DEET, for example) repel a variety of insects and are effective longer than gentler products. I'd rather use a gentler lotion and reapply it as its insect-fighting ability wears off. Trust me, you'll know when that is. If you tuck your pants into your socks and wear long sleeves, you'll be less likely to be bitten by mosquitoes or pick up ticks and spiders. For more than one reason, it doesn't hurt to take a shower right after you come in from the

the spare-time gardener

garden; and when you do, keep your eyes open for pests that hitchhiked their way into your home via your person.

- *Serious footwear.* Whether it's rubber boots with textured soles for traipsing around in the dirt or good sturdy lace-ups to give your foot a good purchase on a shovel top, what you put on your feet can add to your overall comfort in the garden—or expose you to all kinds of potential problems. While those strappy little numbers, "hiking sandals," or even lightweight canvas tennis shoes might look fetching, leave them behind when you go outside to garden.

- *Kneeling pad and strap-on knee pads.* No, these are not just for wimps. Gardening is hard on the knees, so do yours a favor and they'll reward you with many years of service. I also like a kneeling pad that has handles on the ends, so you can hoist yourself up after you've been in one place for a time; and if you turn it over, it becomes a mini-bench. Kneepads with straps that wrap around and fasten at the back of the knee are great. If they have two straps, bottom and top, crisscross them before fastening, rather than running the straps straight across, and they'll stay on better.

- *Portable phone or cell phone.* While there's something to be said for removing yourself from the world's beck and call, most of us can't help wanting to be within reach as much as possible. Taking a portable phone into the garden can save you from an all-too-common scenario: You hear ringing coming from the house, so you leap up from your weeding and take off for the door at a trot, stubbing your toe and tripping over the hose and the cat on your way to the phone—only to find that the caller's hung up by the time you pick up the receiver. And it's probably a good thing, judging from the string of expletives you let loose and the foul humor you're in by the time you reach the phone. If you use a cell phone, put it in your pocket when you head outside, instead of on the kitchen counter; or you can find yourself in the same state of affairs.

AND OTHERS TO MAKE LIFE JUST THAT MUCH EASIER

Here are some supplies, tools, and implements I couldn't do without.

- *Narrow hoe/fork.* This long-handled, two-sided implement probably has some official name, but I just know it as my friend in the garden. One side has two prongs, and the flip side is flat. It works great for weeding or cultivating in narrow spaces while in a standing position.

- *Variable-width rake.* This lightweight, relatively small leaf rake has flexible metal prongs and a lever for adjusting the width of the rake. If you're doing general leaf or grass pickup, use it at its widest. If you're raking leaves or weeds from between plants, set it to its narrowest.

- *Blowtorch on a stick.* That describes a garden tool that's been available for a few years now. My husband's usually the one to wield this petite flamethrower, while I hover over him offering advice: "Don't set the house on fire" or "Watch out for that clematis." It's very satisfying, if a bit gruesome, watching any intolerable grass between bricks and stones crumple up into a little singed mass. Try one; you'll see. What you might not see, though, is the flame, because on a sunny day it's practically invisible. A good solution, which will also help you finish the job sooner, is to do your flamethrowing on cloudy days or at dusk, when you can see the orange flame more easily.

Still, as I tell my husband, "Be careful!"

- *Curved hand fork.* This is great for weeding and cultivating small areas, between plants, say, where a long-handled tool might prove unwieldy. Again, a squishy handle feels good.

- *Half-moon spade.* I use it mostly for edging; and as we know by now, a neat edge gives a great impression and a sense of well-being.

- *Extension pruning saw.* Also known as a long-handled pruner, this may look like a medieval torture device; but it's a handy-dandy item for trimming off branches that are beyond arm's reach. The curved blade cuts in only one direction (towards you). Please be careful.

- *Collapsible trash basket.* I bought one of these at a flower show several years ago and don't know how I ever lived without it. Made of ballistic nylon covering a giant metal spring, this cylinder is perfect for holding really big trash bags. It's light, and even has a strap, so you can carry it around the garden with you. When you're done, just collapse it and secure the fasteners that hold it closed. It stores in no space at all.

- *Leaf discs or bear claws.* These large, flat plastic discs, sometimes shaped to resemble big paws, make it easier to pick up piles of leaves. You can do it with your hands, but it's helpful and quicker to be able to grab such a large "paw full" at one time.

- *Gloves.* I'm not crazy about gardening in gloves. I buy a pair that looks durable and flexible, that molds to my hands through the use of space-age technology; and soon, without even realizing it, I pull them off and throw them on the ground next to where I'm working. Then they get buried and inadvertently tossed out with the garden debris, or saved at the last minute. You can get a much better feel for what you're doing without gloves. Hands are washable, after all. In fact, there are some wonderful soaps specifically for gardeners just like me who don't mind getting their hands grimy but want to know they can clean them off before supper. There is one kind of glove I like to keep on hand, though (a bad but unintentional pun). These ungainly-looking gloves called mud gloves or wet soil gloves aren't particularly flexible, and they're certainly not fashionable like some of the cute little numbers on racks in hardware stores; but they're great for working around plants that are sharpish or for rummaging around in stony soil. They're made of fabric, and the fingers and part of the palm are coated in latex or rubber. Buy them in the brightest colors you can find, and they'll be harder to lose. To wash them, squirt your hands with a hose while wearing the gloves and then take them off and hang them from a peg or clothesline. Storing them inside out prevents putting your hand in the glove only to find that a spider or other creepy-crawly got there first. If you have anything at all in your garden that protects itself with prickles or thorns, another kind of glove you should probably have on hand is a leather work glove. These too are neither supple nor chic, but they'll keep you from getting thorns in your oh-too-tender flesh.

- *Invisible gloves.* There's a new lotion on the market that you spread on your hands before you go out in the garden and use in place of gloves. The beeswax in the mix creates a kind of barrier and prevents staining, and the oatmeal helps moisturize your skin. It lasts several hours, feels good when it's on, and washes off easily with soap and water. It leaves your hands clean and smooth after a stint in the garden and is even said to block poison-ivy oils from reaching your skin. You might want to give it a try.

- *Plant markers.* These come in metal, plastic, ceramic, and wood—the more unobtrusive the better. Anyone with even a modest-sized property knows that it's easy enough to forget where, or even *if,* you've planted something. When you're planting a whole swath of a familiar plant, don't worry about a marker; after all, you're not running a botanical garden. But if you have a perennial bed, or perennials mixed in with shrubs and annuals, marking them can make all the difference between identifying valuable green shoots and mistaking them for weeds.

- *Maximum–minimum thermometer.* It's helpful to know how cold it was overnight and how warm it gets during the day. These thermometers aren't terribly expensive, and they can help you plan your garden year by letting you know when it's consistently warm enough at night to start planting. Since we're all in our own little ecosystems, your numbers may be far different from those the weather gurus predict, or even those they report after the fact.

- *Rain gauge.* Giving your garden too much or too little water can lead to several different kinds of problems. If you know how much rain you've had, you can plan and water accordingly, and a rain gauge is the easiest way to be sure how much precipitation there's been. They come in many designs. Some mount on a fence post or other architectural element, and some are attached to a stake in the ground. When you buy a rain gauge, make sure it's serviceable, and position it where the measurement won't be affected by roof overhangs, bushes, or other obstructions. Then don't forget to read it, and empty it before the next rainy day.

- *Roll of twist ties.* These can make tying up plants a snap, since you "snap" them off from the roll by means of the little cutter included on the framework.

- *Storage on the go.* Several years ago, as a birthday gift, I received a garden "tool belt" that fastens around a five-gallon utility bucket. There's a top on the bucket, which serves as a seat. This great gift is a lightweight organizer for small garden implements, seed packets, extra trash bags, markers and plant labels, and all the other little items I use when gardening. What doesn't fit in the pockets can go under the lid. It means fewer trips to the garage or basement, and *that* means time saved.

- *Apron.* A plain old carpenter's apron with pockets is handy, too, although it can be tough kneeling down if you try to carry tools in its pouches.
- *Notebook.* A contractor's notebook that has several compartments and can close up tight is fine for carrying smaller items, as well as a pencil or pen and paper that will later become pages in your garden notebook. If it's drizzly, you can keep paper out in the damp only as long as necessary and then tuck it inside the case.
- *Folder.* Lately, in a megastore, I found a useful item called a forms folder. It's probably meant for use by bureaucrats or accountants; but it looked like it might be handy in the garden and didn't cost much, so I bought it. It's a metal clipboard backed by a plastic container I can use for notebook pages, seeds, stakes, etc. It's small and light and, so far, indestructible.
- *Zone map.* The U.S. Department of Agriculture's multicolored Plant Hardiness Zone Map might not be considered a tool or implement, but it's certainly important to your gardening success. Once you know your planting zone, as determined by the USDA's calculations of the range of minimum annual temperatures, you'll know which perennials you can grow. Although the map has been broken down not only into zones (1 through 10), but also further into subzones (5a and 5b, for example), being aware of your number is generally enough. Once you know your zone, you can use it when planning your garden, and subsequently whenever you're shopping for plants or getting ready to plant. Keep one of these maps near your gardening tools or where you plan your garden. They're frequently included in gardening catalogues and magazines. The National Arboretum's website (www.usna.usda.gov) has the map and some valuable information to go with it.

KEEP IT CLEAN; KEEP IT WORKING

I know we're trying to save time in the garden, but maintaining your tools has to be done. One way is to keep a bucket of builders' sand (the coarse kind, also useful for sandboxes) with just a little leftover motor oil in it. Hose off the worst of the dirt from your tools, and when they're dry, plunge them into the oily sand and move them around so the abrasive material will do its work.

AND . . . NOT WORTH THE MONEY OR SPACE

There are some tools on the market that are simply not worth the investment in money or garage space, and some even squander your hard-earned time.

Take weeders, for instance. Some seem to have been dreamt up by inventors who were frustrated that the rack and other instruments of torture have fallen out of favor. The consumer twists and turns handles within handles and pokes and prods the lowly dandelion, armed with the promise of a perfect lawn. These elaborate instruments seldom work as well as simpler tools and instead are a testament to the strength and tenacity of the weeds they're meant to eradicate. Don't waste your money.

When it comes to planting bulbs, dibble at your peril. Dibbles—those contraptions that are basically tapered, hollow metal tubes about ten inches long—are meant to ease the job of planting bulbs. Ideally, they remove just the right amount of soil so you can insert the bulb and then release the soil to cover it. Some have inches calibrated on their sides so you'll know how far down to plant the bulbs. There are models with flanges to make pushing them into the soil easier, and still others with hand-lever systems that help release the soil.

Neat, huh? Generally, what they do is remove a core sample of soil that looks worthy of a paleontologists' attention, and then hold onto it jealously so you have to use yet another implement to extract the soil to cover the bulb. Or the soil crumbles as you try to get it out of the hole in the first place, and then where are you? The hole's filled up before you get a chance to plop the bulb into it. For an easier way, see chapter 27, "Planting Your Purchases." If a tool is ultra-specialized, or too complicated, or takes up too much room, pass it by. It can only bring grief to you and your wallet.

the spare-time gardener

35

oh, deer! and other critters

As much as we love to look at wildlife, we like it to keep to itself. Deer and skunks are particularly adept at invading rural or suburban gardens and dining on our expensive and beloved plants. I've seen elk roaming through a small city in Canada, chomping on the shrubbery as they made their way from backyard to backyard. During mud season in Maine, moose tend to gnaw on nice new shoots and leave very deep tracks in the ground as souvenirs; and blackflies and mosquitoes vie for the title of "State Bird."

There are chemical deterrents for most creatures that pester gardeners, but it's important to make sure they aren't toxic to children and pets, not to mention adults.

DEAR SWEET DEER

Deer seem to be the most common source of gardeners' woes. These marauders can strip trees and shrubs and wreak havoc in the perennial border; they also facilitate the spread of disease-bearing ticks.

Some of the methods people use to discourage deer are downright creepy. Do you really want human hair, or worse, sprinkled around your garden? Do you have the time to spend on dubious deterrents?

The surest way to keep deer out of your yard is to erect an eight-foot-high fence (can those deer ever jump!). While it might not look good on a suburban front yard, the flexible, dark-plastic mesh deer fencing made today can blend right into the edges of some backyard landscapes. In the long run, it's probably easier than trying method after method and renewing and re-spraying time after time. A pass-through incorporated into the fencing can make your yard accessible to you and yours but inaccessible to your deer friends.

Even a normal picket fence might convince the deer to go next door for their supper rather than leap into your yard.

If fencing isn't an option, you might like to try some of the following:

- Lights and sprinklers triggered by motion detectors. These may work for a while, but they lose their effectiveness when the deer become accustomed to them.
- Dry repellent that comes in fertilizer form. When added to the soil, it may keep deer away for up to two years.
- Foil plates that sway in the breeze and mylar ties on bushes. These aren't terrifically attractive, and they also lose their clout with time.

- If you can stand them, sprays made of eggs and water (recipe below) or from the "juice" of hot peppers. You'll have to renew these weekly or after every rain, whichever comes first.
- Commercial sprays made with soap, along with materials unattractive to deer. These have more staying power, so you can wait several weeks between applications.
- Some plants are as truffles and foie gras to deer (e.g., hostas and daylilies), but others make them lose their appetite. If you plant enough of the latter, the deer may decide to go elsewhere for their hors d'oeuvre.

Perennials we're told deer will leave on their plates include monkshood, bugleweed (ajuga), artemisia, lily of the valley, bleeding heart, foxglove, ostrich and cinnamon ferns, bearded and Siberian iris, lavender, lupine, poppies, mature peonies, and lamb's-ears. They're also not crazy about daffodil and hyacinth bulbs.

In the shrub and tree department, deer are said to avoid bayberry and bittersweet, birch, red cedar, cotoneaster, larch, lilac, redbud, and redwood. There are plenty of annuals that don't whet their appetites, including alyssum, candytuft, lobelia, nicotiana, and snapdragons.

ROTTEN EGG SPRAY— A DETERRENT FOR DEER (AND PROBABLY PEOPLE, TOO)

Blend or whisk together 1 large egg and 2 cups of water. Pour this into a one-gallon container with a lid (you'll need it!). Add 10 cups of additional water, and mix well. After two days, use a garden sprayer to apply this mixture to foliage that the deer find attractive, and reapply every week or after it rains.

SKUNKED AGAIN

Aside from the obvious olfactory disadvantage of having skunks in your yard, there's the lesser-known fact that they love to dig up bulbs and other tasty morsels. To some of these, grubs for instance, we say good riddance; but others cause us to say, rid us of these skunks. Here are some tips:

- Don't leave pet food on your porch or steps. If you do, your local skunk (who thinks he's a cat) will stop by for a meal, and when the dog barks at him will thank you the only way he knows how.

- If you have a bird feeder, try to keep the area under it cleared of birdseed as much as possible. Skunks love snacking.

- If you have fruit trees, pick up any windfall so the skunks won't try to make applesauce or peach jam on your lawn.

- Using bonemeal to fertilize bulbs is like putting up a sign that says "Good Eats." Some people plant their bulbs in clumps and then cover the clump with a piece of wide-mesh screening, and some even put their bulbs in wire cages—way too much trouble. Plant more bulbs than you think you need; then consider the few bulbs you might lose as the price to pay for having a garden that wildlife admire as much as you do. Daffodils, mentioned above as a food deer will leave on their plates, don't seem to appeal to skunks or rodents either.

- Think about borrowing or buying a humane trap to capture "forest felines," opossums, raccoons, or other pesky critters; and then transport them to more hospitable surroundings (*not*

your local golf course). Check the instructions for ways to keep yourself safe and prevent skunks from letting loose in your car.

- Rabies is a serious subject—and can be a serious menace. Don't take any chances. If in doubt about an animal that's hanging around your property, call your local animal control officer; and never get within nipping distance or try to handle any wild animal, no matter how docile it appears.

BUGS AND SLUGS!

Some of the nastiest creatures you'll encounter are barely visible, either because they're tiny or because they're so well camouflaged. What to do? Here are a few suggestions.

- Slugs, those slimy, brown snails-without-shells, make lace out of our leaves. There are some products on garden center shelves that promise to rid us of these disgusting blobs, but one solution may be in your laundry room: mothballs. Sprinkle these around your garden to repel slugs, skunks, and other animals. Another way is to put out a small bowl or shallow can of flat beer so the rim is at ground level and then wait. Fish out the dead (or simply passed out?) slugs in the morning and toss them. You can also go out at night with a flashlight and sprinkle salt on them and then get the satisfaction of watching them squirm, knowing they'll soon be goners. It's a little macabre, but maybe you're *that* mad at them.

- Mosquitoes, blackflies, and other biting insects can be kept at bay to some degree with special clothing, sprays, lotions, and candles or incense. Lavender and citronella are said to be repellents. We swore by "punk" sticks when I was a child, partly because they had a nice "punky" smell. They're still on the market.

- I hate earwigs. They're just plain creepy; even their name is enough to give me goose bumps. They can also do real damage to your plants. Since they like damp, dark places, tightly roll up a few sheets of newspaper, run water on the paper for a few seconds, and then put it in your garden. Early the next day, go out with a plastic bag and, gingerly but quickly, dump the newspaper into it, using a tie to secure it really well. Put the bag in the trash. The next day, try again. To keep earwigs out of your house, cut back branches that touch or nearly touch the building and do what you can to keep damp areas

the spare-time gardener

to a minimum. That will help control mold and mildew, too.

- To annoy whiteflies and aphids, use the most environmentally neutral insecticidal soaps you can find, or make your own with dishwashing liquid or liquid hand soap.
- Plant native species that have evolved to resist the predations of local pests. These plants are generally happier in their surroundings than imports, so they'll be stronger and better able to fight off onslaughts by diseases, as well as insects.

MOLES, MICE, AND THEIR RELATIVES

Try to eliminate prime nesting and living areas by eliminating piles of brush, grass clippings, and leaves. In the garage, be careful how you store piles of utility cloths and towels, birdseed, and other materials attractive to critters. If you buy your dog and cat food in bulk, store it in a container made of plastic or metal, not cardboard. Sprinkling mothballs around your garden and near any rodent tunnels you see might convince them to relocate elsewhere in the neighborhood.

OUR FRIENDS IN THE GARDEN

There are some animals that are beneficial. These you may want to encourage by planting their favorite foods and offering them low-cost housing. The price: They rid your yard of unwanted pests, till the soil for you, or simply look good.

Arachnids

Spiders, of course, are good because they trap insects in their intricate webs. On the other hand, they seem to do just fine without any assistance from humans. One way you can help them help your garden is to just let them do their thing. If a web isn't too obtrusive, admire the artisanship that went into making it, as well as the bugs wrapped up in silk for later snacking, and leave the spider's universe undisturbed. Inside the house, however, let your conscience be your guide.

oh, deer! and other critters

The Birds and the Bees— And Bats

Birds, bees, and bats are beneficial in their own ways. They should be encouraged to take up residence—at a safe distance. You don't want any of them showing up in your living room (like the night a bat swooped in immediately after a "Dracula" movie ended); and you want to limit your contact for safety reasons.

While birds might want to feast on valuable earthworms or on your newly planted seeds if you go the seed-planting route, they also eat lots of insects, grubs, and other creatures that harm our gardens. Instead of, or in addition to, keeping a well-stocked birdfeeder, invite your avian friends to visit or move in by providing plants with berries and seeds that birds like to eat to supplement their diet, houses appropriate to the species you'd like to attract, and even materials to help them build their nests (bits of fluff and twigs).

Present birds with a diversity of plant sizes, shapes, and types. At ground level, they like to turn up insects in lawn and garden. Shrubs become a medium-height, protected perch—a stopping place between the lawn and the treetops. Tall trees provide nesting sites, and evergreens of all heights offer cover, as well as protection from winds year-round. If any of these plants have edible berries or seeds, all the better.

If you have cats that are allowed outdoors, you should limit your efforts to attract birds. The temptation will just be too great for your resident hunter to resist, not that a cat would even want to resist the thrill of the chase; and then you'll feel guilty when kitty comes home with a beautiful bird clamped proudly between his or her jaws.

Without bees there would be precious few flowers. These beneficial insects pollinate blossoms by flitting from one to another with little bits of pollen on their legs. While this is purely a by-product of their other activities, it makes them VIP residents of our gardens. If you find yourself in need of a serious hobby, you might want to take up bee-keeping. Or better yet, encourage your neighbors to tend a hive or two.

Bats do humans the favor of consuming unimaginable numbers of insects every night. For that they're to be praised and encouraged. They generally do just fine living in trees and drafty barns but, unfortunately, on occasion find their way into our homes. There are specially made wooden "condos" available if you want to try to attract a bevy of bats. Just don't try to make friends since they're sometimes rabid.

More Creatures

Ladybugs are cute, until they start appearing in our homes by the hundreds and expiring on the windowsills in little orange clumps. The ladybugs you find outside eat aphids and do no harm to people. You can actually purchase them and release them into your garden, and it's said that dill and its relative, Queen Anne's lace, attract them. There are ladybug houses on the market, too; but whether they really need our help to fly away home is questionable.

Butterflies are remarkably beautiful, and watching them "flutter-by" is always mesmerizing. You can encourage them to visit your garden by including certain plants in your landscape. Keep in mind, though, that the caterpillars that eventually become butterflies are voracious eaters. Host plants on which butterflies like to lay their eggs, and which later become food for the newly hatched larvae, include herbs and vegetables such as cabbage, parsley, dill, and milkweed. If you see their caterpillars, why not move them to a plant on which they can happily feast without incurring your wrath?

To attract visits by butterflies, perhaps those that have hatched elsewhere, include nectar-bearing plants with flowers that make good landing areas, are brightly colored, and are heavily perfumed. Buddleia or butterfly bush, cosmos, monarda or bee balm, rudbeckia, and zinnia are a few.

part five

Garden Odds and Ends

36

latin in the landscape— putting in a good word for a dead language

Latin may be defunct as a native tongue, but it's been alive and well in horticultural circles ever since 1753. That's when the inventor of botanical Latin, Carolus Linnaeus of Sweden (known to family and friends as Carl Linné), published *Species Plantarum*. While he and others had taken a stab at naming plants before then, this definitive publication listed and categorized all the plants known to Linnaeus and established the rules of botanical nomenclature.

Some people wear this arcane language like a badge of honor and can get pretty tedious about using it and pronouncing it "correctly" (as if they were around in Ancient Rome!). Nonetheless, most seri-

ous gardeners believe that knowing a plant's Latin name(s) can come in very handy, and some plant labels and catalogues skip the common names altogether. Since our ultimate goal is to make life easier and help our gardens flourish, it's a good idea to pay attention to botanical Latin. The, ahem, "right" way to pronounce it is a matter of custom—and opinion.

PLANT LATIN 101

While we all use ordinary, garden-variety names for plants, some of these designations can be pretty fanciful. Moreover, you need only look at all the different plants called by one name (lilies, for example) to know that a single word can describe a bevy of totally unrelated plants. Conversely, one plant can have many names or nicknames.

Not so with botanical nomenclature, as it's called. One plant, one Latin name; it's that simple.

Every single plant that's ever been identified has a Latin name. Much of botanical Latin consists of non-Latin words that are "latinized" to fit into the descriptive system Linnaeus devised. Some of these names are etched forever in stone. However, the International Botanical Congress meets every five years, and once in a while the powers that be decide to change a name for scientific purposes, update it if you will . . . but that's another story.

So what's the lesson here, and how can it save you time? Basically, if you check out the Latin name on a plant tag or in a catalogue description, and then match it up with what you know about botanical nomenclature, in many cases you can easily and quickly determine a plant's characteristics—color, size, habit, and other features. If there is no Latin name listed, be wary of your source; you could be getting just about anything.

Once you get to know some of the descriptive terms, you'll have a good idea of what any given plant wants to be when it grows up. And that will allow you to help it reach its full potential.

GENUS AND SPECIES— DEFINING THE PLANTS

In what Linnaeus called the binomial system of nomenclature (in latinized Swedish, we can only assume), the first word in a botanical Latin name is the plant's genus, or generic name. The second word, the species name, or specific epithet, narrows down the description. The generic name is a noun, and the specific epithet is an adjective.

The word *Rosa* to indicate a plant's genus or generic name at the beginning of a botanical name means that the plant is a true rose. *Syringa* is lilac; *Ilex* is holly (there are 350 species of *Ilex* alone!); and so on for every genus.

In the binomial system, the second word in the name (the specific epithet) indicates the species within a genus by describing a plant's characteristics, origins, or preferred habitats. *Rosa rugosa*, therefore, is a specific kind of rose, actually a rough or wrinkled rose; and *Rosa multiflora* is another species of rose—one with many flowers. *Syringa vulgaris* is the common lilac. *Allium tuberosum* is garlic chives: *Allium* is the garlic genus; the *tuberosum* means fleshy underground.

the spare-time gardener

There are many of these descriptive words, and they're used over and over again, tacked onto many a genus. And, just to confuse matters, their suffixes have to match the gender of the first word—the genus name. So one plant's species is *rugosus* and another's is *rugosa,* while yet another's is *rugosum;* and there are plenty of exceptions to that rule— you don't want to know!

In deciphering these species adjectives, you can basically ignore the suffix and consider its root. You'll find that some of the meanings are intuitive; *purpureus* (or *purpurea* or *purpureum*) means purple, and *vulgarus,* etc. mean common. See, this is easy.

Genus and species names can be a version of the name of the individual who first discovered or developed the plant, sometimes an esteemed botanist or horticulturist. The genus in honor of John Stewart, therefore, became *Stewartia.* Trying to pronounce some of these latinized proper nouns can result in some scholarly conundrums, since many contain sounds no self-respecting ancient Roman ever uttered.

The botanical names can also refer to a location where the plant was first discovered or characteristics of the plant, such as coloring, shape, size, etc. *Solidago canadensis* is goldenrod (*Solidago*) that was discovered in Canada (*canadensis*).

In descriptions, you'll often see a plant's scientific genus name capital-ized and italicized: *Rhododendron* refers to a particular species vs. rhododendron if you're taking a more generic view of the plant. This second word is italicized but not capitalized, as in *Cornus kousa* (kousa dogwood). *Cornus* is the dogwood genus; *kousa* is a Korean species. Often, the capitalization is maintained but the names aren't italicized.

If you see a third word or set of words, it's the name of a particular variety or cultivar and defines the plant still further. Whether they're in botanical Latin (written in italics) or English (written in single quotes), these terms usually describe the plant in some way and set it apart from others in its species. One more example: *Lavandula angustifolia* 'Rosea' is the lavender genus, a species with narrow leaves (*angusti* = narrow; *folia* = leaf), and a variety or cultivar with pinkish flowers. See how the second and third words end in "a" to agree in gender with the genus *Lavandula.*

Just to make botanical nomenclature even more interesting, there's often an abbreviation or an "x" thrown into the mix. The "x" (really a multiplication sign) indicates that the plant is a hybrid. The letters "cv" mean it's a cultivated variety, and "var" means variety. "L." means that Linnaeus himself was the source. Sometimes in a catalogue you'll see a heading for a particular genus, say *Acanthus,* and then to save space, the various species available will be listed below as *A. hungaricus* (Hungarian acanthus) or *A. mollis* (soft-haired acanthus). There now, that's "cc"—crystal clear—isn't it?

This really isn't as daunting as it seems. Pay attention as you thumb through garden catalogues or check out plant labels. Once you start seeing these terms over and over, you'll get the hang of it. Moreover, having a basic understanding of botanical Latin will help you save time deciding which plants to use—really it will.

GENUS (A.K.A., GENERIC NAME)

Since scientific names are often used at garden centers and by landscape experts, it's helpful to have at least a nodding acquaintance with the botanical Latin for some of the most popular flowers. Below are genus names followed by the common names of some plants you're likely to see. For a great many, though—Rhododendron, Hydrangea, Zinnia, Clematis, to name only a few—the scientific and common names are the same.

Achillea = yarrow
Antirrhinum = snapdragon
Aquilegia = columbine
Campanula = bellflower
Convallaria = lily of the valley
Cornus = dogwood
Dicentra = bleeding heart
Digitalis = foxglove

Gypsophila = baby's breath
Helianthus = sunflower
Hemerocallis = daylily
Hosta = plantain lily
Ilex = holly
Kalmia = mountain laurel
Lilium = Asiatic and oriental lilies
Mertensia = bluebells
Monarda = bee balm
Lavandula = lavender
Paeonia = peony
Pelargonium = annual geranium
Philadelphus = mock orange
Primula = primrose
Rosa = rose
Rudbeckia = black-eyed Susan or cone-flower (*Echinacea* is also called cone-flower)
Sedum = stonecrop or hens and chickens
Syringa = lilac
Viola = violet or pansy
Zantedeschia = calla lily

SPECIES (A.K.A., SPECIFIC EPITHET)

This is a list of a very few of the useful species names—the second word in the plant name. This is just to get you started, so you'll get the gist of botanical Latin.

albus (alba, album) = white
arboreus (arborea, arboreum) = tree (watch out; it will get big)
argenteus (argentea, argenteum) = silvered
aurantiacus (aurantiaca, aurantiacum) = orange

aureus (aurea, aureum) = golden

azureus (azureua, azureum) = light blue

biflorus (biflora, biflorum) = double-flowered (twice your money's worth)

caeruleus (caerula, caeruleum) = medium blue

carnosus (carnosa, carnosum) = fleshy (usually good for dry areas)

compactus = low and round (good for smaller gardens)

cyaneus (cyanea, cyaneum) = darker blue

durabilis (durablis, durabile) = sturdy, durable (a good choice)

dys = bad (beware on many levels)

foetidus (foetida, foetidum) = odiferous (be careful with these)

lilifolius (lilifolia, lilifolium) = lily-leaved

luteus (lutea, luteum) = yellow

maximus (maxima, maximum) = largest (wow!)

officianalis = medicinal (but you wouldn't want to eat it without a doctor's say-so)

purpureus (purpurea, purpureum) = purple

repens = creeping (useful as a ground cover)

roseus (rosea, roseum) = pink

rubens = red

spinosus (spinosa, spinosum) = spiny (watch out for these around children)

velox = fast-growing (do you have the room?)

venustus (venusta, venustum) = handsome (how nice)

vernalis (vernalis, vernale) = spring-flowering (useful to know when shopping)

viridis (viridis, viride) = green

PRONUNCIATION— WE THINK

Don't fret if you can't pronounce every single botanical name. If you take a little time to learn the basics and then pay attention when the pros speak about plants, you'll be in clover. Just promise me you won't become a plant snob after you become fluent in botanical Latin.

Here are a few "rules" to help you get started:

- Pronounce every vowel.
- Accent the next-to-the-last syllable (most of the time).
- Pronounce "ch" as you would "k" in kite.
- The pronunciation of "g" is also hard, as in girl.
- Pronounce "ae" as "i" in kite.
- Pronounce "eu" as "oy" in toy.
- Pronounce "ou" as in clout.
- When names of people and places are used, they should be pronounced as in the original: Virginicus, for example, is pronounced like the state but with a "cus" at the end.

If you want to learn more than the smattering in this chapter, or more than you can glean by hanging out with gardeners or at your local nursery, why not check out a book on this new old language?

37

the gardener's seasons

The year may be broken up into strictly defined seasons that start and end on specific times and dates, but gardeners know better. Throughout history and all over the world, gardeners and farmers have recognized and named the quirky, unpredictable times that don't strictly follow the calendar's divisions. They've planted by nature's seasons and abided by nature's rules. Rather than feeling hemmed in by the calendar, gardeners can revel in the opportunities open to them throughout the year.

What follows is a collection of arcane facts, just for fun, sprinkled with a few tidbits of useful information.

MANY MOONS AGO

Did you know that every full moon has a name? In fact some have several. While this knowledge probably won't add much to your gardening skill, or save you time in the garden, it does make good conversation.

Most of the names were bestowed by Native Americans and reflect their mythology and seasonal experiences. These vary according to tribe and location. Not to be outdone, European settlers provided their own monikers for some of the moons. Try to imagine the derivations, and then take your pick of the ones you like. Of course, the Native Americans didn't have desk calendars to tell them when January was turning to February, so some segues from one month to another are blurred.

- January—Stormy, Wolf, or Snow Moon (or Moon after Yule—a European addition)
- February—Snow or Hunger Moon
- March—Sap, Crow, Crust, or Worm Moon (or the European Paschal Moon)

- April—Sprouting Grass, Egg, Full Fish, or Pink Moon
- May—Flower, Corn Planting, or Milk Moon
- June—Strawberry or Rose Moon
- July—Thunder, Hay, or Buck Moon
- August—Harvest, Green Corn, Red, Grain, or Sturgeon Moon
- September—Coon or Harvest Moon
- October—Acorn or Hunter's Moon
- November—Frosty or Beaver Moon
- December—Long-Night Moon or Cold Moon

BLUE MOON—MORE THAN A SONG TITLE

Since the lunar month is just under 30 days long, the full moon appears on different days each month, and sometimes twice in a month. That second full moon is known as a "blue moon." Once, flying into Philadelphia late in the afternoon on December 31, I saw the brilliant orange sun setting off to the left side of the plane precisely while, at exactly the same height, the full "blue" moon was rising on the right—a memorable moment.

There's undoubtedly something special about all full moons, blue or not. Mythology and mystery aside, though, your palest plants will simply glow by the light of the moon. Don't miss the show.

IN SPRING

Since spring is many people's favorite time, let's begin the year in the garden with spring. This is indeed the season of hope. In early spring, after the snow has melted (at least temporarily), I don't actually *do* much in the garden. What I do instead is *peer* at the garden—at the bare ground—and simply *will* those green shoots to burst through. When they do, it's cause for great rejoicing.

"Look," I'll announce, "the daffodils are coming up! The violets too!" It's a joyful moment, and it was just as happy an occasion in Pennsylvania—a zone or two further south—as it is in Maine. Spring is spring, and it's a new beginning, wherever you are.

That's one of the finest things about perennials and bulbs. Every spring, year after year, you can anticipate their arrival and experience the exhilaration of seeing nature at work. And it is indeed work for those little shoots struggling to breathe free; but, with a genetic predisposition to reach for the sun, they manage admirably. Once one leaf or sprout arrives, they all seem to follow suit quickly; and before long you have a garden.

Annuals are a part of every great and appealing garden, but perennials are the backbone—and they're what will keep you from going stir crazy as spring begins. Get to know what your perennials and bulbs look like in their infancy so you won't plant something on top of them or, worse still, pull them out.

Early spring is the time to start seeds, if you'd like to have that pleasure and have the time. It's also a good time to cut some expendable branches from your flowering trees and shrubs for forcing into bloom inside. Forsythia and fruit trees are the classics. Advice about complicated methods abounds; but for these plants, simply put them in water and watch them leaf out and flower.

It's uncanny how if March comes in like a lion, it goes out like a lamb, and vice versa. Whoever came up with that expression knew what was what. Spring may officially begin with the vernal equinox, but sometimes it takes some real faith in Mother Nature to believe it.

In the old days in Maine, the expression "climbing the March hill" referred to getting through what was economically the toughest month of the year. If you were going to come close to starvation before spring, this might be the time. Psychologically, we still climb the March hill towards spring and the golden days of summer. At least it's the month when the maple syrup comes into its own.

To paraphrase Percy Bysshe Shelley, if April comes, can spring be far be-

hind? Generally in April, at least in New England (and particularly in Maine), the deep frost begins to melt and it rains a great deal. All the soil turns sodden and viscous. We slog around in this for about a month and shrug it off saying, "Mud season's here. Oh well, at least it's spring." Duck shoes are a must at this time of year. Fortunately, the mud usually dries up before the influx of tourists—and we don't tell them about it.

Southerners have their own problems in April. Just when they let their guard down, up crops Blackberry Winter—the name for an unexpected cold spell. These are inevitable, but infrequent enough to be infuriating. Fortunately, it doesn't last. As soon as it's out the door, plant your garden!

What do you feel like shouting when your plants freeze one last time in late spring? May Day! Pay attention to the zone map, but remember there's always the exception to the rule. Check out a seven-day forecast before you do your first planting, just to give yourself a better chance of avoiding a freeze. What could be worse than having to plant everything twice?

Digging in the Dirt

In spring, finally, peering at the earth can give way to working it. I have some good news for procrastinators, though. If you're one of us who don't always get around to cutting back every last plant at the end of the season, or raking up every leaf, you are now in luck. Those brown and withered stems and leaves are protection when a cold snap ignores the weather map. Don't pull them back too early. Wait until the weather's more conducive to outdoor work and planting.

A word of warning, though: There's a fine line between benefit and detriment when those old plant materials lie atop the new shoots. Uncover them too soon, and the new shoots shiver and suffer; uncover them too late, and the poor things are pale and wan and way too leggy than is good for them. In addition, after they're up more than an inch or two, raking around the new growth becomes increasingly hazardous to your plants' health. You can end up with ragged, holey leaves for the rest of the season.

Now's the time when a lot of us want to turn over the soil in garden beds. Another word of warning: Since overusing automatic tillers can mush everything together into nasty, homogenous clumps, ruining your soil's structure, even if you have an area that simply won't respond to anything but mechanical tilling, please don't do any more than is absolutely necessary. And don't do it at all until the ground has dried out a good bit.

Once you keep your journal for a year and have notes and drawings of where everything is planted, spring will be an even more exciting time. You can compare this year's notes to last year's. You'll know what's coming up, as well as where and when. Sure, this takes away some of the element of surprise—but there are plenty of other surprises waiting for you.

Nip That Impulse in the Bud

Now, of course, is when the planting bug is at its most virulent. You want to start buying plants, and lots of them. You want to dig in the dirt. You want to tool around with your wheelbarrow. Hold that thought—unless it's to treat yourself to the makings for that one bright cheerful container.

Do your homework and your reconnaissance first. Then, and only then, should you head to the nursery for your major plant purchase of the spring.

Another boon for procrastinators: Waiting before planting can get you safely by that unexpected frost, when those who were too hasty lose some of their plants—and have to spend the time to buy more and start planting all over again.

Planting According to Nature

While you should pay attention to the zone maps, the odd thing is that many

of us have mini zones on our properties. So, when you're choosing plants,
think of those south-facing areas where
you can go a zone higher, and those
shady hollows where you have to shave
off a zone or two when planning and
planting the garden.

This applies to planting dates, as
well. You have to decide whether you
want to stretch the limits by planting
before the last frost date for your area.
Because I'm afflicted with spring fever,
I like to put in store-bought plants that
I know are pretty sturdy (pansies and
primroses, for example), but I'll wait
before putting in the more tender
species.

Maintenance

Spring is the time to repair and renew
the rickety garden furnishings and less
than perfect tools you put away in a fit
of pique last fall.

IN SUMMER

The summer solstice, welcomed by one
and all, is on June 21, not long before
Midsummer's Night—but summer
seems to start before that. Maybe it's
wishful thinking. Summer is my other
favorite season in the garden. It's when
everything that's going to flourish
flourishes. It's also when you can tell
which plants aren't going to make it and
still have time to replace them.

June is when the appropriately
named "bangsashes" appear. These
plump and crunchy flying blimps are
better, and just as appropriately,
known as June bugs. No matter how far
north you live, it's safe to plant your
garden this month. Finally!

July is the time for fireworks, both
those made by nature in the form of
thunderstorms and those made by
human hands. In the colder regions of
the country, there's a saying: We have
two seasons here—winter and the
Fourth of July. Variations abound, but
what they all mean is enjoy July while we
have it.

If you're going to experience "the
dog days of summer," they're probably
going to be in July; and salad days are
here, literally. Let's hope you're in the
midst of your very own "salad days,"
thanks to a few homegrown veggies.

August can be a drier, less buggy
version of July; in other words, perfect.
For that we love it. With dryness, of
course, come plants that turn brown
unless we water them, talk of droughts
and water conservation, and a feeling
that summer's o'er. Alas. Cheer up:
Fall brings crisp air and fewer weeds.

IN FALL

This is my favorite season—*outside* the
garden. The weather's great. Up until
December, those of us in severe denial
can still believe that winter is a ways

away. After you've used your journal to take stock of the season just past, it's time to put the garden to bed (I love that expression).

While you don't have to go overboard (remember when you're raking that a covering of leaves is helpful for your overwintering perennials), keep in mind that every tenacious weed you pull now is one less you'll have to deal with next spring, when you'd rather be planting and tending the plants you love. Grass that's growing amidst your flowers and shrubs will only grow stronger and spread out; so if there's any left, make the time and tug it out.

Another reason to get rid of the detritus is to improve your garden's hygiene, so to speak. Even beautifully tended gardens have some pests, and the best way to ensure they or their offspring don't winter over in comfort, only to reappear hale and hearty in the spring, is to get them out of there. Let them live at the dump! You don't need them; you don't want them.

Plant diseases like to simmer away under garden debris too. Save yourself the trouble and expense of replacing favorite perennials by cutting off old stems now, rather than waiting till spring. Simply pull out annuals by the roots, shake the soil off into the garden, and get rid of them.

Clearing out the garden is a chore that often gets overlooked, and about which we can procrastinate no end; but even if you can only rid yourself of a portion of the garden trash, you'll be a few steps ahead the coming April or May.

Even though you get to know what your plants look like as they emerge in the spring (flat spears for daffodils, whorled nubs for violets and columbines, chunky spears for hostas), it isn't always easy to tell which green sprout is something you want in your garden, and which is a nasty weed. Now's a good time to make sure plants are labeled, and then get out that garden notebook again and make sure the last plants of the growing season are recorded there. Some of these are likely to appear later in the spring, and wouldn't it be a tragedy to pull them out, thinking they're weeds.

Prices Fall in Fall

Nursery owners don't want to provide living space and care for leftover plants all winter, so they often put a lot of their inventory on sale in the fall. This is a perfect situation for procrastinators, not only because they'll save a little cash *but also because this is the best time to plant a lot of perennials.* If you put them in the ground now, allowing them a little time to get settled in before winter's first assault, they'll be fine and will be back to greet you in the spring. In many ways, waiting is better for the plant than, say, planting it in midsummer heat, when you run the risk of not providing enough water.

Maintenance

While September brings some of the best weather of the year, the autumnal equinox also ushers in even shorter days and, in the north, the possibility of an early frost. There's still plenty of time to enjoy your garden, and even better, there's less to do. That isn't to say your work in the garden is finished for the year, though.

In the north, October often brings the first snow of the season—a reminder of what's to come. It's time to tuck the garden in for the winter. Generally in October (or November, depending on where you live), a string of warm, sunny—in other words, perfect—days arrives. Indian summer is a glorious chance to enjoy the warmth one more time before winter closes in. It was also a Glenn Miller hit record and, in an even less politically correct world, was called Injun Summer.

Overseas, there are different terms for our Indian Summer. Geese seem to play a prominent role. In Germany, it's *Gansemonat* (Goose Month); and in England, this is Goose Summer, an expression that gave rise to "gossamer," a name for a gauzy fabric that looks like cobwebs in the garden. In Russia, there's a time in the fall called Women's Summer because women who work in the fields are given a respite.

If you haven't already done a final pickup in your yard, November may be your last chance till spring. Once the ground freezes, protect woody perennials by piling on any mulch you have left over, as well as any evergreen branches you've collected.

You can plant bulbs until the ground freezes. Little exemplifies hope and faith in the future like planting bulbs in the fall. We dig a hole, plunk what looks like an onion in it, cover it up, and bide our time. The bulbs' timing is perfect. Just when we think we can't stand another colorless day of winter, they appear and proudly announce they were worth the wait. More and more of them will come up year after year. Is that not the perfect kind of plant?

This may be a time for planting bulbs, but it's also a good time to start planting not-so-subtle hints about all the garden implements and gift certificates to nurseries you'd like for the holidays.

IN WINTER

Winter has its compensations. Just when you begin suffering from cabin fever, the spring plant catalogues begin to sprout in your mailbox. Open them; revel in them; and order from them (if they have something that fits into your Planting Plan). They are a welcome sign of things to come.

Snow is protection for overwintering plants. While you shouldn't pile wet, heavy snow on woody perennials and shrubs, if possible leave a good layer of snow over the garden as long as possible. In other words, save yourself some time and trouble and don't go overboard with the shoveling.

Your roof, unfortunately, is a different story. Snow falling off roofs in great, loud, swooshing clumps can severely damage the plants below. If necessary and possible, use a roof rake to take the snow off your house in smaller increments. Some people swear by electric tape tucked under the roof shingles near the edge. While we've found that this can prevent ice dams and water damage inside the walls, the best way to protect plants is to keep them out of harm's way. Plant them away from the drip line—or in this case, the snow swoosh line.

If you use a fireplace or woodstove, save the wood ashes to spread around your plants in the spring.

While you can force bulbs you purchased back in the fall and have subjected to a period of steady cold temperatures, it's easier (although a littler more expensive) to wait until late winter or early spring and then purchase bulbs someone else has primed for you to the point where they're ready for forcing. When you receive them, pot them immediately, set them in bright light, give them a little water,

and watch them sprout and burst into fragrant bloom.

During the time of year we call December, our earliest ancestors cut and brought in evergreen boughs, and of course the holly and the ivy. The winter solstice reminds us that in spite of the cold days ahead, the days are getting longer. Celebrate New Year's in the traditional way, with a look back and another ahead—and give a thought to your garden's past and future, too.

At some point in the winter, there always seem to be a few days of sun and warmth that melt a lot of snow and ice—the January thaw. This often causes some nasty flooding, an experience to which I can personally attest. Remember the old expression of hope: Lord willin' and the creek don't rise? That was probably coined in January. Not coincidentally, pundits have decreed that the most depressing day of the year is in this month.

What's to be done? Remember that the hours of daylight are increasing day by day. Keep your face turned to the sun, when it's out. And remember what my Scottish grandfather was wont to say: "When January's done, winter's back is broken."

February is our shortest month— and a good thing, too. Its function is to test our endurance before March, when spring officially arrives. All it's good for is thumbing through catalogues and planning the garden—and, oh yes,

Valentine's Day! Houseplants need a lot of TLC at this time, too.

If Punxsutawney Phil, or any less vaunted woodchuck, sees his shadow on Groundhog Day, it means six more weeks of winter. Or is it the other way around?

In late winter, just when we really need it, there will be a day that presages spring. We'll be heartened by a little sun and a patch of grass showing through the snow cover. We'll feel the warmth and know there's hope for all of us. Of course, gardeners are especially fortunate. In one way or another, we can find hope in *every* month and *every* season.

38

now, with all your
newfound spare time . . .

If you use the ideas in this book—and others you've discovered for yourself—you might, on occasion, find yourself with more spare time than you expected. If you're as busy as most of us are, you'll have no trouble filling the void; but I heartily recommend rewarding yourself for all your hard work.

You can surely come up with many ideas for enjoying free time in or around the garden, but here are just a few suggestions.

One simple but effective reward: Pour a nice cup of tea or your libation of choice, have a seat in a comfy lawn chair, and enjoy your garden—as a spectator. If you see any weeds or plants that need deadheading, ignore them! They'll still be there tomorrow. Open a good book. Relax.

A VISITOR IN YOUR OWN GARDEN

If you want to work around your plants but are so up-to-date with your garden chores that your green thumbs are simply itching for something else to do, here are a few suggestions.

- Eat your flowers! Blooms you can put in salads or serve as garnish include violets, marigolds, Johnny jump-ups and pansies, and those peppery nasturtiums. I've been told that tulip flowers are delicious, and I can vouch for the good taste of deep-fried daylilies. Just dip them in a light batter of 2 beaten eggs, 1/2 cup of flour, and 1 tablespoon of milk; season as desired with salt and pepper; and sauté them in olive or canola oil. You can make buttery shortbread cookies or scones dotted with luscious nuggets of your own lavender. It should be dried before you use it in recipes. Other flowers should be served fresh out of the garden.

You can sugarcoat violets by dipping the blossoms in beaten egg whites and then in superfine sugar. If you shape them as you go and then dry them, they'll look just like a more glamorous version of themselves tucked around cakes and other desserts. It goes without saying, but I'll say it anyway: Never serve any flowers that have been treated with herbicides or pesticides.

- Pick some flowers and interesting foliage and dry them. First, select specimens that are not too bumpy, so they'll flatten well. Then, spread them on a square you've cut from a brown paper bag, and cover them gently with another piece. Put them under a pile of books or something else flat and heavy. After several days, remove your newly dried plants and sandwich them between sheets of clear laminating paper, glass or other materials, or simply paste them on as is to make greeting cards, bookmarks, or framed decorations.

- If you want a regular bouquet of dried flowers, simply buy some drying compound in a craft stores and follow the directions. Easier still, tie small bunches of flowers and herbs and hang them upside down in a warm, dry, well-ventilated area until they're nice and crispy.

- Arrange some of your own flowers in one (or better yet, several) of the many vases you have cluttering up your shelves and display the fruits of your labors. Do not be intimidated by three-inch-thick tomes on flower design. The easiest way to go wrong is by trying too hard to make an "Arrangement." Instead, simply cut flowers you like, keeping their stems all about the same length, and put them in water-filled containers that please or amuse you. Using your artist's eye, adjust the lengths to suit the vase and the look you want—tall and airy or short and compact. A little greenery can help soften the edges but isn't strictly necessary. It's proportion that counts here, and with just a bit of practice (and paying attention when you see combinations you enjoy), you'll get a feel for the colors, textures, and sizes you like, and how best to combine them. Fresh flowers look wonderful in just about any combination, so don't fret. Remember, this is a reward.

• Use your plants to craft decorations for your home. Make a wreath of living succulents, ferns, or coleus, or a dried wreath of hydrangea heads you can let dry right on the plant. Make easy sachets of dried lavender or other herbs or flowers. To make wreaths, use a round frame and other materials specifically made for that purpose. They're available at any crafts store, and the employees in such stores are generally knowledgeable and enthusiastic about crafting and can give you helpful tips.

• For a living wreath, tuck a liberal amount of slightly moist sphagnum moss into the frame and wrap it into place with wire. Gently insert the plant materials using a skewer or large toothpick until the look is full and lush. Keep it moist, and it will look great for weeks (be careful you don't hang it on something that will suffer from the moisture).

• For the hydrangea wreath, simply tie the blossoms on the form with flexible wire made for just that purpose. Or mass the blooms in a low vase or pot—no watering necessary.

• For sachets, purchase little gossamer bags, fill them with dried herbs or flowers, and tie them with ribbons. If you're handy with a sewing machine, fashion bags by cutting out two small rectangles of fabric and sewing them together on three sides. Turn the piece inside out, cut the raw edge with pinking shears, fill it with dried blossoms, and tie with ribbon. This method works for pillows and hotpads, too. The variety of crafts using dried and fresh flowers and foliage is unlimited.

• Feed the birds. Put out a suet cake, orange halves, or pinecones slathered with peanut butter. Hang a birdfeeder, and keep it filled. Some are even "guaranteed" to keep out squirrels. If you'd rather not have to worry about the fields of unwanted sunflowers or millet that can sprout up under bird feeders, you can sterilize the seeds. To make feeding easier during the growing season, instead of putting out commercial bird feed, plan your garden so it includes plants with flowers, nuts, berries, and seeds that appeal to birds while brightening your view.

• Take artistic photographs of your flowers and little scenes within your garden. Compose your photos as painters do: Think of Georgia O'Keefe's large-scale close-ups or Childe Hassam's gentle garden portraits. Frame them, name them, sign them, and exhibit them at a local art show. Maybe you'll sell your work, and you might even win a prize. Wouldn't that be a grand reward for the time you put in on your garden? You can go out and buy some plants!

- Use some of the herbs you grow to make delectable dishes. There's nothing like fresh salsa made with your own cilantro, omelettes made with your own chives, pesto from your own basil, or ice tea with a sprig of your own mint. Just use your imagination, and you'll be thrilled with the results.

- Make customized stepping stones for your garden. Find a mold that's big enough for your purposes and the shape you want—a deep, plastic tray; dishpan; deli container; what have you. Buy a bag of ready-to-mix, quick-setting cement. Now, in a spot where you don't mind making a mess (use a tarp or newspapers anyway), don a dust mask and dump half the bag, or as much as you want to use, into a big plastic bucket. Mix in the proportional amount of water called for on the bag, and stir it with a big kitchen spoon until it's well mixed.

Spread it in your mold, smooth the top with the back of the spoon, and when the consistency is thick enough (but not too thick), make impressions in the cement with objects, hands, leaves, whatever strikes your fancy. When you become adept at getting the mix and the timing right, you can write sayings on the stones with chopsticks. After a couple of days, or when the mix is totally dry, pry the stepping stone out of its mold, dig a depression in the soil so the stone will sit at ground level, and gently tap it into place. You can make as many of these as it takes to create a charming, individual pathway— or, if you use handprints, your own walk of fame.

- Sit in a comfy lawn chair and page through catalogues until you find the perfect hammock, and then order it. Hang it up, either between two trees or on a stand. It will provide a great spot from which to survey your new and improved leafy-green kingdom.

OUT OF THE GARDEN AND AWAY FROM HOME

- Purchase a simple, natural-looking fountain. Decide beforehand whether you want to use it outside. If so, it should be labeled as

the spare-time gardener

suitable for outdoor use, and you should be able to plug it into a properly grounded outdoor outlet without the use of extension cords. Wash and arrange some interesting small stones in the bowl (now you know what to do with some of the pebbles you've dug from your garden), and surround it with ferns and other plants that like humidity. You can even include some water plants; more and more nurseries are stocking plants for water gardens. Fill the fountain with water, plug it in, sit back and close your eyes. Voila! A Zen experience.

If you're feeling ambitious, it's fun and easy to build your own fountain using favorite or found objects and a small recirculating pump. You can find instructions online, or the salespeople at a garden center that sells pumps and accessories will gladly help.

- Attend a hands-on horticulture workshop at a botanical garden, an adult education program, or a garden club class. You'll learn new skills, hear other gardeners' ideas, and meet like-minded neighbors. Better yet, volunteer at a botanical garden or arboretum, where you can not only learn about the plant world through docent training, but also share your newfound talents.

- Gather together a few friends and visit gardens and take garden tours. What fun you'll have!

index

the spare-time gardener

about the author

After eight years as an award-winning reporter for the *Boothbay Register*, **Barbara Hill Freeman** joined the staff of Coastal Maine Botanical Gardens, where she serves as director of communications. She continues to write for newspapers, magazines, and the CMBG newsletter. She shares her office with a 2,000-volume horticulture library and people who live and breathe gardens. Becoming a Master Gardener through the University of Maine, Freeman took the required forty-plus hours of class time and provided more than the minimum forty hours of volunteer time, with additional instruction and volunteer time in subsequent years. She has tended gardens in Pennsylvania, Florida, and Maine and knows the requirements of various climates. She has visited and written about many gardens, including those of celebrities as well as of avid home gardeners. She is a Perkins Gardens Trustee for Wave Hill in Bronx, New York. Freeman was awarded the First Prize in Environmental Reporting from the New England Press Association in 2000 and has received numerous awards for writing and photography from the Maine Press Association. She lives a few feet from the Atlantic Ocean with her husband, Ned, and their menagerie of a big, hairy dog and three fine cats.